The Birth of a Nation

The Birth of a Nation

THE EARLY YEARS OF THE UNITED STATES

Doris Faber and Harold Faber

CHARLES SCRIBNER'S SONS • NEW YORK

Charles Scribner's Sons Books for Young Readers
Macmillan Publishing Company
866 Third Avenue, New York, NY 10022
Collier Macmillan Canada, Inc.

Printed in the United States of America
10   9   8   7   6   5   4   3

Library of Congress Cataloging-in-Publication Data
Faber, Doris, date.
    The birth of a nation: the early years of the United States/Doris Faber and Harold Faber. — 1st ed.
    p.   cm.   Bibliography: p.   Includes index.
    Summary: Examines the important events and figures involved in the first federal government to the election of John Adams as the second president.
    1. United States—Politics and government—1789–1797—Juvenile literature. [1. United States—Politics and government—1789–1797.]
I. Faber, Harold. II. Title.   ISBN 0–684–19007–9
E311.F33 1989   973.4—dc19   88–30805   CIP   AC

CONTENTS

PREFACE

In 1789, a great political experiment was about to begin—
the creation of the first government of the new United
States. Two years earlier, delegates gathered at Philadelphia
had written a constitution outlining an unprecedented federal system, and after bitter political argument it had been
formally ratified. But how were its noble aims actually to be
put into operation?

This question posed a challenge without any parallel.
Never before had an entirely untried government sprung
into existence, based only on a piece of parchment. None of
the foundations of the federal establishment as we know it
today had yet taken shape. There was no president, no Supreme Court, and the new Congress envisioned by the Constitution scarcely resembled the Continental Congress
functioning under the old Articles of Confederation.

Indeed, the Constitution's framers had sought new solu-
tions for the failure of that first attempt by the former colonies to cooperate for national purposes. Nobody could be

sure, of course, whether the new government would work effectively. Nevertheless, the extraordinary caliber of the leadership available—especially the universal assumption that George Washington would be the first president—gave strong grounds for hope.

Two hundred years afterward, the success of the great experiment may seem hardly surprising. Yet we tend to forget that the political pressures affecting a simpler society were not too different from those of today, and knowing this can make the future seem less daunting. Today, as the United States faces a range of atomic problems undreamed of by the Founding Fathers, it is important to remember that the birth of the nation was not easy.

Who were the important figures involved? How did they fashion a working government out of the ideas and ideals set forth in the Constitution? What issues did they face during the country's formative years? And the country itself—what was it like in those early days of the American republic? To answer such questions is the purpose of this book.

The Birth of a Nation

1

We the People

ON A COOL MORNING LATE IN SEPTEMBER OF 1788, the first wagon train of emigrant families moved out over the new Cumberland Trail, which linked the Blue Ridge Mountains of North Carolina to the West. Ahead was a dangerous trip of one hundred and eighty miles through the lands of the Cherokee Indians, already angry about the advance of white settlers into their home country. Because of the danger, the state furnished the new settlers and their families with an armed escort of sixteen men.

Among the armed men in the party was a new official eager to bring law and order to the wilderness of North Carolina—twenty-one-year-old Andrew Jackson. Just admitted to the bar as a lawyer, he had been appointed district attorney of the western district of the state. Being on the side of the law was something new for Jackson, who had earned a reputation as a wild young man while growing up in North Carolina. According to one local resident, "Andrew Jackson was the most roaring, rollicking, game-cocking, horse-racing, card-playing mischievous fellow that ever lived in Salisbury . . . the head of the rowdies hereabouts . . . more in the stable than in the office."

Lanky, with intense blue eyes and a long face marked by a scar that ran into his ruddy hair, Jackson was fiercely independent, always ready to fight if he felt it necessary to defend his honor. He had received the scar as a boy in the Revolutionary War when, at the age of thirteen, he had served as a mounted orderly for the American forces. Captured by the British and ordered by an officer to shine his boots, young Andy had refused. The officer lifted his sword and struck Jackson on the head, inflicting a gash that left him permanently scarred.

After the war, Jackson—an orphan by then—spent a wild few years, involved mainly with horses and horse racing, before he decided to study law in the office of a local attorney. Upon being admitted to the bar, Jackson sought an opportunity to try his luck in the West, where land was open for the taking and there were few lawyers.

On his way, he often had to prove his valor. One night along the trail, Jackson alerted his party to an impending Indian attack. When the Indians found the wagon train prepared, they melted back into the woods. Another night, Jackson shot a panther as it was trying to kill one of his horses. After nearly a month on the dangerous journey, the group he was escorting reached the crest of a bluff overlooking the Cumberland River. Below them he saw Nashville—consisting then of two taverns, two stores, a distillery, and one log courthouse, surrounded by a fringe of cabins, tents, and wagon camps. From that rude outpost, in 1789 Jackson began a career as a lawyer and military commander that would lead many years later to his election as president of the United States.

In the year the nation was born, thousands of Americans like Jackson were on the move. By foot, by horseback, by oxcart, and by boat, they kept pressing westward. A Massachusetts newspaper, the *Salem Mercury*, reported that a gentleman returning from Kentucky had met a single party numbering 1,004 people bound for the wilderness there, and one small town in Pennsylvania counted 236 wagons laden with men, women, and children passing through on the way to Ohio.

Although some of these travelers were already Americans, many had only recently come from Europe to the United States. Because Europe offered no open land and little work while the New World promised both land and work, it was no wonder that tens of thousands fled across the ocean. From the beginning, the United States was truly a nation of immigrants.

The earliest arrivals had included various groups seeking religious freedom, such as the Pilgrims who came to Massachusetts or the Quakers who originally settled Pennsylvania. But over the years, more of the newcomers had been driven by poverty to look for economic opportunity in America. Some left the cities of Europe as indentured servants, trading four years of labor for a chance to make a new life. Others sold their few belongings and took themselves and their families across the ocean hoping to buy land and become independent. And there were others who came involuntarily—black slaves from Africa and convicts from England.

Understandably, the first arrivals had taken possession of land along the coast, usually near rivers, where they started farming. In the North, around the Saint Lawrence River and the Great Lakes, trapping beaver and other animals for their skins became a major occupation. Many New Englanders earned their living by catching fish off the banks of Newfoundland. In the South, with its warmer climate, owners of large plantations, dependent on slave labor, grew rice and tobacco near the tidewaters of the major rivers, while small independent farmers developed more traditional crops farther inland.

In both North and South, later arrivals found themselves unable to acquire coastal land for farming, so they began moving to the interior, where often the soil was not as rich. In quest of better prospects, the next wave went farther west, buying land from speculators or merely "squatting" on it, assuming ownership of the land just by taking possession of it. Only rarely did the settlers go through the formal procedure of buying land from the Indians who lived on it, because most of the pioneers considered that the Indians were merely heathens with no rights at all. One of the newcomers summed up the prevailing opinion: "It was against the law of God and nature that so much land should remain idle while so many Christians wanted to labor on it."

This attitude did not make life easier for the pioneer settlers, who were frequently attacked by hostile Indians, angered at the invasion of their lands. The newcomers also faced many other problems in striving to make a living in the wilderness. To convert forest into farmland meant cutting down trees by ax and then removing the stumps, no easy task. Even after a crop was planted, months elapsed until it could be harvested, and meanwhile a family had to eat. To survive, pioneer men became skilled hunters, shooting deer, wild turkeys, and even squirrels for food. Pioneer women were equal partners, preparing food, making clothing, gathering nuts and berries, and raising children.

How many people were there in the new United States? And where did they live?

Those questions can be answered with more precision

than might be expected because 1790 was the year of the first census taken in the United States. When the count was completed, at a cost of $44,377, the nation's population was put at just about four million—3,929,204, to be exact, a little less than in the city of Detroit today.

At that time, the United States consisted of only twelve states, but when Rhode Island, the last of the thirteen original states to be admitted to the Union, did enter, its population was included in the total. So was the population of Vermont, which became the fourteenth state in 1791. Maine and Kentucky, which were still parts of Massachusetts and Virginia respectively, were counted separately during the initial census.

Geographically speaking, the United States that began functioning under the Constitution in 1789 was, of course, much smaller than it is today. By the terms of the peace treaty of 1783 with England, the new country included 827,844 square miles, about one quarter of its present size. Bounded on the north by the Saint Lawrence River and the Great Lakes, it stretched south to Georgia between the Atlantic Ocean on the east and the Mississippi River to the west.

Across the wide Mississippi, the vast Louisiana Territory and the area that was later to become the plains, mountain, and Pacific coast states belonged to Spain. To the north, a hostile England retained possession of Canada—and still occupied some forts within the United States near the Canadian border, reluctant to yield them even though she had agreed to do so in the treaty of peace. To the south, East and West Florida were colonies of Spain.

Though the area covered by the 1790 census was comparatively small, the census takers, who were court marshals, encountered great difficulties. In many localities there were no roads, and where roads did exist they were usually in poor shape, frequently impassable because of mud or snow. Only a few bridges had been built, so crude ferries were the only means of crossing many rivers. Transportation was almost entirely by horseback and took much longer than most people today might guess. For instance, a journey from the banks of the Potomac River, where George Washington lived, to New York required eight days under favorable weather conditions, longer if it rained.

Nevertheless, the census takers somehow managed to complete their work and reported as follows:

STATE	POPULATION
Vermont	85,425
New Hampshire	141,885
Maine	96,540
Massachusetts	378,787
Rhode Island	68,825
Connecticut	237, 946
New York	340,120
New Jersey	184,139
Pennsylvania	434, 373
Delaware	59,096
Maryland	319,718
Virginia	747,610
Kentucky	73,677
North Carolina	393,751
South Carolina	249,073
Georgia	82,548
Southwest Territory	35,691
TOTAL	3,929,204

But that total was not really complete. For one thing, American Indians were not counted; they would not be officially counted as part of the American population until 1860. Moreover, no count was made in the Northwest Territory—the area taking in the present day states of Ohio, Indiana, Illinois, Michigan, and parts of Minnesota—although settlers were already pouring into the region. And, as in any census, many people everywhere were missed for a variety of reasons.

When the returns were finally tabulated, Thomas Jefferson, who supervised the census as part of his duties as secretary of state, wrote, "Making very small allowance for omissions, which we know to have been great, we may safely say we are above four million."

Despite its flaws, the tally sheets of the first census do give a picture of the American people during the nation's first years. They show, for instance, that the population of the young nation was about 80 percent white and 20 percent black. Almost one-fifth of all the people—754,208—were blacks imported from Africa, or their descendants, about the same percentage as in the United States today. But one big difference must be noted: 90 percent of the blacks, or 694,697, were slaves at that time.

The white population was counted in three different categories. The first was "free white males" over sixteen years of age, deemed to be the primary source of military and industrial manpower—813,365. The second category, white males under sixteen, totaled 802,077. The third group, white females of all ages, added up to 1,556,628. Altogether, the male population exceeded the female by 58,814. In addition, the first census showed an average family size of 5.7 persons, about twice what it is today.

From the census we know, too, that most of the family

names in the nation were of English and Scotch origin, with many Dutch names in New York. One authority says that 75 percent of the white Americans of 1789 had come from England or were descended from emigrants from the British Isles, 8 percent from Germany, and the others from France, the Netherlands, and Spain.

Of all the ethnic groups in the United States at that time, the single most important was the Scotch-Irish. Driven by economic pressures from Scotland first to northern Ireland and then to the United States, the Scotch-Irish had poured first into Massachusetts and then into Pennsylvania. Back in the early 1700s, a Philadelphia observer noted: "It looks as if Ireland is to send all its inhabitants hither, for last week not less than six ships arrived and every day two or three arrive also."

Many Scotch-Irish males became typical frontiersmen— adept with the long rifle and ax, proud and independent, and ready, like Andy Jackson, to fight at any time. Another notable characteristic was their suspicion of the politicians and merchants of the East they had left behind. In almost every state, the backwoods settlers of the western areas had real grievances. They were underrepresented in their state legislatures, and they were frequently unable to convert their products such as grain or whiskey into cash to pay tax collectors. Another sore point was their contention that the government gave them insufficient protection against hostile Indians.

This sort of dissatisfaction had resulted in an armed protest in 1785. Farmers in western Massachusetts, angry at the seizure of their cattle and lands for failure to pay taxes, took part in what came to be known as Shays' Rebellion, after Captain Daniel Shays, their leader. The revolt, put down by force the following year, demonstrated how much discontent existed throughout the land among small farmers, who constituted a majority of the population. One historian has said that posterity should thank Daniel Shays because his uprising caused many of the delegates who met in Philadelphia in 1787 to be more favorable to the idea of a strong national government than they might otherwise have been when they wrote the new Constitution.

During the fight over ratification of the Constitution, the differences between easterners and westerners became increasingly obvious. In South Carolina, inland farmers were disturbed by the fact that all four of their state's signers of the Constitution were aristocrats from the seaport of Charleston. In Pennsylvania, all eight of those signing the Constitution came from Philadelphia, regarded by the western settlers as a city of moneylenders and oppressors of agriculture. Thirty-five of the thirty-nine signers of the Constitution lived adjacent to salt water, clear evidence that the farmers of the interior were not adequately represented.

And geography inevitably affected the world outlook of the American of that day. Easterners looked toward England and France for trade and culture. Many of them sent their sons to England for education; they had representatives in London to sell their crops and handle their money. Westerners, however, felt much less direct connection with Europe. Because of the barrier created by the Appalachian Mountains, they found it easier to send their crops down the Ohio and Mississippi Rivers to New Orleans, controlled by Spain, than to the East. Control of the Mississippi River was a paramount political goal for the westerners, something easterners could not understand.

For the westerners, the Constitution represented a new attempt by the eastern elite—the merchants, the moneylenders, the speculators—to retain control of their lives. They saw the new strong central government as a threat to the rights of a free people and to the more representative state governments. In many states, there were more people opposed to the new Constitution than for it. The closeness of the ratification vote illustrated that: New Hampshire, fifty-seven for, forty-six against; Virginia, eighty-nine for, seventy-nine opposed; New York, thirty for, twenty-seven against. The major reason the Constitution was adopted in those states was a promise by its supporters to amend it as soon as possible with a bill of rights to protect citizens against the federal government.

Despite political differences, however, Americans everywhere did accept the new Constitution. They looked eagerly toward New York, the city chosen as the nation's capital—at least, for the time being—where the actual organizing of the new federal government was about to begin.

2

The First Congress

IN 1789, NEW YORK CITY was a city of elegance and of crudeness. Men and women of the upper classes dressed in the latest fashions from London or Paris to go to balls in their horse-drawn carriages. Yet the streets were not lighted, and pigs ran wild on them. The hog nuisance was so bad that one rhymester wrote in a newspaper:

> Oyes! Oyes! Oyes!
> This is to give notice
> To all Hogs, Pigs, Swine and their Masters
> That from the first of February '89
> If any person suffer his, her or their swine
> To gallop about the streets at large.
> Full Twenty shillings is the charge
> For each offense
> To be paid (by firm and special order)
> To Our good Alderman and Recorder
> To the informer's use and all expense;

> Otherwise, he shall be free to dine
> Upon said arrested swine.

At that time, New York was the second largest city in the nation, with a population of about 28,000, slightly less than that of Philadelphia. By modern standards it was small, covering only the southern tip of Manhattan Island, but it was a thriving port, growing fast. It had twenty-two churches, a hundred and thirty-one taverns, five newspapers, one theater, six livery stables, and about four thousand houses. There were no paved roads, few sidewalks, and no indoor plumbing; each house had a privy outside. For heat, people used fireplaces or Franklin stoves.

Even in those early days of New York, before the growth of the stock markets, the most important street in the city was Wall Street. Not only was it the center of political life in the United States, it was also a fashionable place to live. Alexander Hamilton lived at 58 Wall Street. Nearby were the homes of many other lawyers. One of the best boarding houses in the city, in those days before hotels, was that of Mrs. Daubigny at 15 Wall Street. Several new members of Congress lived there, not far from Federal Hall, the new home of the first Congress of the United States.

Once New York's city hall, Federal Hall had been renovated for the new Congress under plans drawn by Major Pierre L'Enfant, the French-born architect who had served as an American army officer during the Revolutionary War. Later, he would be charged with designing the new city of Washington, D.C.

Federal Hall was described by one writer as the largest and most elegant building on the North American continent. Under L'Enfant's plan, a striking stone facade at the corner of Wall and Broad Streets embodied several designs using thirteen stars as symbols of the former colonies that had become states. The most prominent of these depicted an American eagle holding a shield and clutching thirteen arrows in one claw and an olive branch in the other, symbols of war and peace.

With no regrets, the old Continental Congress, a debating society that had little governing power, went into oblivion. But before it did, it provided a timetable for the election of the new Congress and the first president of the United States. It set the first Wednesday in January, 1789, for the selection of electors for president in the various states, the first Wednesday in February for the meeting of the electors to cast their votes for president, and the first Wednesday in March as the date for the new government to begin operations.

In those days before television, radio, and daily newspapers, elections were quite different from today's. For one thing, candidates did not campaign for office. There were no political conventions, no speeches, no political polls, no mailings, no appeals for funds. But the biggest difference was that few people voted, because voting was a privilege reserved for well-off white men.

Although the setting of voting qualifications was among the powers reserved for the states, a brief experiment allowing women to vote in some parts of Virginia and New Jersey during the American Revolution had already been generally condemned as too radical. In keeping with the prevailing idea of denying any political role to women or blacks, voting was restricted not merely to white men, but to white men who owned property. As a result, almost all those who were candidates for office belonged to the elite top-level of society known as the gentry. They were well off, well educated, and firmly convinced that the business of government should remain in their hands. One of their greatest fears was "anarchy," a condition of lawlessness, which the privileged few felt would be the inevitable result if the uninformed and uneducated public were allowed to make political decisions.

Despite that fear, in the momentous first national election early in 1789, there was unanimous agreement among the elite as well as the masses of the people about who should be the first president of the United States—George Washington. Indeed, quite probably the new Constitution, with its broad powers for the new office of the presidency, would not have been adopted or ratified if everybody had not expected that Washington would be the first president. Everywhere, he was looked up to as a hero because of his role as the commander in chief during the American Revolution.

Still, political differences certainly existed among the American people. Although the nation was quite small, with a population of scarcely four million, political passions were as powerful then as now. The people seemed almost evenly split between those who felt that a strong national government would provide the only way to preserve independence and those who believed just as fervently that state governments, which were closer to the people, were the best protectors of their rights. That split was reflected in the votes to ratify the Constitution, which passed by only a narrow margin in several states. While there were no organized political parties then, those who supported a strong national government had become known as Federalists and those opposed as Anti-Federalists.

During that very first election, the opposing sentiments were expressed with vigor. Up in New Hampshire, for instance, one center of political talk was the tavern operated by Captain Ebenezer Webster, an old soldier who had served with General Washington at the battles of Ben-

This famous portrait of George Washington, the so-called Thomas Chestnut portrait, was painted from life by Gilbert Stuart. *Collection of the Architect of the Capitol; Library of Congress.*

nington and White Plains. For Captain Webster, the issue was absolutely clear: If Washington supported the new Constitution, then so did he. And if Washington was available to be the new president, there could be no other choice. Captain Webster's young son, Daniel Webster, sitting in a corner listening avidly as his father expounded the Federalist position, would grow up to be one of the Union's staunchest defenders in the United States Senate.

Captain Webster spoke out with such energy that he was chosen as one of New Hampshire's five electors in the nation's first presidential race. He got on his horse one cold morning—the first Wednesday in February of 1789—and rode to Concord, the state capital. There he surprised nobody by proudly casting his ballot for George Washington. Every other presidential elector did the same in New Hampshire.

Elsewhere, however, things were different. In New York, the two opposing political factions were so evenly divided that they could not even agree on how to select electors to vote for president. As a result, no electors were chosen, and New York did not cast any ballots in the first presidential election.

During the same period, members of the first Congress also had to be picked, with similar political maneuvering attending their selection. In Virginia, James Madison, known even then as "the father of the Constitution," was defeated for election as that state's first senator because of opposition led by Patrick Henry, the leader of the Anti-Federalists there. Madison then ran for a seat in the House of Representatives and was elected by the voters of his district.

In other states, however, the voting proceeded normally, with senators being chosen by the various state legislatures, as provided for in the Constitution, while members of the House of Representatives were elected by the people. Then the new members of Congress slowly made their way by horse, stagecoach, or boat to New York, for the opening ceremonies of the new government.

The old Continental Congress had set March 4 as the date when the members of the new Congress would take their seats. But nothing much happened on that day. Only eight members of the Senate and thirteen of the House of Representatives appeared—not enough to make a quorum in either chamber. Bad weather and travel difficulties kept other members from arriving on time.

Day by day for weeks, additional members kept turning up. Fisher Ames, a representative from Massachusetts who had appeared promptly on the first day, wrote angrily to a friend in Boston: "We lose credit, spirit, everything. The public will forget the government before it is born." Other members of Congress wrote pleading letters to their absent colleagues, requesting their attendance, but it was not until April 1 that a quorum was achieved and the House of Representatives finally began to function.

Its first order of business was to elect a presiding officer, called the Speaker of the House. Frederick Augustus Muhlenberg of Pennsylvania, a clergyman who had turned to politics, won the post and took his place in an ornate chair, below a sculpture depicting the spirit of liberty. In front of him, desks and chairs were arranged in a semicircle for the other members. Above and behind them, galleries for the public overlooked the large and impressive chamber.

Muhlenberg, then forty-nine years old, had been a member of the Continental Congress besides having presided over the General Assembly of Pennsylvania and the Pennsylvania convention that ratified the Constitution. While he had earned a reputation for being impartial, actually he was elected because of geography. Since George Washington came from Virginia and John Adams, the prospective vice president, came from Massachusetts, many members felt that the large and influential state of Pennsylvania should also be honored.

It took the Senate almost a week longer, until April 6, to achieve a quorum. On that day, it elected John Langdon of New Hampshire as its chairman for the sole purpose of officially counting the ballots cast by the nation's first electors for president and vice president. A fifty-eight-year-old merchant, Langdon had distinguished himself as a civilian in the Revolutionary War by helping to finance the Continental Army and by leading a body of militia to the Battle of Saratoga in 1777, before the British surrendered there.

Langdon occupied the presiding officer's chair at one end of a crimson-draped room smaller than that of the House of Representatives, but no less imposing. Its ceiling was adorned in the center by a carved sun surrounded by thirteen stars. Senators sat in a semicircle of chairs and desks, facing a raised platform at the front. But there were no seats for the public because the Senate held its sessions in secret for its first five years.

With Langdon presiding and members of the House of Representatives also in attendance, the returns of the first presidential election were formally counted. Of course, then as now, everybody already knew how each of the states had voted and so the results were no surprise. But the election was not official until the ceremonial counting.

By the original terms of the Constitution, each elector had two votes. The person receiving the largest number would become president; and the one receiving the second highest, vice president. Here is how the tally went in 1789:

STATE	WASHINGTON	ADAMS	OTHER
Connecticut	7	5	2
Delaware	3		3
Georgia	5		5
Maryland	6		6
Massachusetts	10	10	
New Hampshire	5	5	
New Jersey	6	1	5
Pennsylvania	10	8	2
South Carolina	7		7
Virginia	10	5	5
TOTAL	69	34	35

As soon as the figures had been read out, Washington was officially declared elected president unanimously and Adams Vice president. Ten other candidates received a scattering of votes. It should be noted that electors from only ten of the thirteen states actually voted. North Carolina and Rhode Island were still ineligible to vote because they had not yet ratified the Constitution, and New York was so split that it had failed to select any electors for the presidential balloting.

Nevertheless, the provisions of the Constitution had been satisfied—and Congress immediately took action toward carrying out the electoral mandate. Langdon dispatched an agent—Charles Thomson, secretary of the Senate—to inform Washington of his election.

While awaiting Washington's arrival, which could not be expected for several weeks, the House of Representatives set to work on other matters. On April 8, James Madison arose and proposed a bill that he described as "of the greatest magnitude": to raise funds by a tax on imports of rum, molasses, wine, sugar, coffee, tea, and other goods into the United States. In the debate that followed, there were disagreements about the rates of the proposed import tax, but no one disputed the necessity of raising revenue for the new government.

Not only was the import tax passed in time to start raising money that summer, but its passage also marked the emergence of Madison as the leader of the House. Only thirty-seven years old, Madison had already made a reputation for himself at the Constitutional Convention and in the fight to ratify the Constitution.

Physically frail, Madison was a small man, not much more than five feet in height, but his learning and diligence in addressing complicated subjects led many other able men in Congress to follow his guidance. By common consent, his fellow representatives entrusted the direction of the business of the House to him, and he soon became the most influential man in Congress.

During that period, the Senate largely marked time. It deferred to the House on the tax bill, as provided for in the Constitution. Under the Constitution, the Senate had been set up as a more deliberative body than the House, insulated somewhat from the public. Senators had to be at least thirty years of age, in contrast to twenty-five for members of the House; they were elected for six-year terms, instead of two years as in the House; and they were elected by state legislatures instead of directly by the people, as House members were.

Who were the members of the first Congress?

Fisher Ames of Massachusetts described them this way: "There are few shining geniuses; there are many who have experience, the virtues of heart and habits of business." About a third of the members of each house had studied law.

Almost half of the senators were landowners or planters, as
were 36 percent of the representatives. Merchants made up
17 percent of the House and 14 percent of the senate. The
average age of a representative was 43.5 years; of a senator,
46.1 years.

Almost all had previous political or governmental experience. Senator Richard Henry Lee of Virginia had introduced
the motion that led to the Declaration of Independence in
1776. Representative Roger Sherman of Connecticut was the
author of the basic compromise governing the states' representation in both houses that had made the Constitution possible in 1787. Representative Robert Morris of Pennsylvania
was known as "the financier of the Revolution" for his work
in raising funds to support the Continental Army.

Many of the first members of Congress have been forgotten, but they should be remembered. For it was they, together with George Washington, John Adams, Thomas
Jefferson, and Alexander Hamilton, who established the
foundations of the American government as we know it today. Only eleven states were represented in the first session
of the first Congress because North Carolina did not ratify
the Constitution until November 21, 1789, and Rhode Island
until May 29, 1790.

Here then are the names of the members of the nation's
first Congress:

THE FIRST SENATORS

NEW HAMPSHIRE: John Langdon, Paine Wingate.
MASSACHUSETTS: Caleb Strong, Tristram Dalton.
CONNECTICUT: William S. Johnson, Oliver Ellsworth.
NEW YORK: Rufus King, Philip Schuyler.
NEW JERSEY: William Paterson, Jonathan Elmer.

PENNSYLVANIA: William Maclay, Robert Morris.

DELAWARE: Richard Bassett, George Read.

MARYLAND: Charles Carroll, John Henry.

VIRGINIA: Richard Henry Lee, William Grayson.

SOUTH CAROLINA: Ralph Izard, Pierce Butler.

GEORGIA: William Few, James Gunn.

THE FIRST REPRESENTATIVES

NEW HAMPSHIRE: Nicholas Gilman, Samuel Livermore, Abiel Foster.

MASSACHUSETTS: George Thatcher, Fisher Ames, George Leonard, Elbridge Gerry, Jonathan Grout, Benjamin Goodhue, Theodore Sedgwick, George Patridge.

CONNECTICUT: Benjamin Huntington, Jonathan Trumbull, Jeremiah Wadsworth, Roger Sherman, Jonathan Sturges.

NEW YORK: John Laurance, Egbert Benson, William Floyd, Peter Silvester, John Hathorn, Jeremiah Van Rensselaer.

NEW JERSEY: Elias Boudinot, James Schureman, Lambert Cadwalader, Thomas Sinnickson.

PENNSYLVANIA: Henry Wynkoop, Frederick Augustus Muhlenberg, Daniel Hiester, Thomas Scott, George Clymer, Thomas Fitzsimons, Thomas Hartley, Peter A. G. Muhlenberg.

DELAWARE: John Vining.

MARYLAND: William Smith, George Gale, Daniel Carroll, Joshua Seney, John Sevier, Michael Jenifer Stone, Benjamin Contee.

VIRGINIA: Alexander White, James Madison, John Page, Richard Bland Lee, Samuel Griffin, Andrew Moore,

Josiah Parker, Theodorick Bland, Isaac Coles, John
Brown.

SOUTH CAROLINA: Thomas Tudor Tucker, Aedanus Burke,
Daniel Huger, William L. Smith, Thomas Sumter.

GEORGIA: Abraham Baldwin, James Jackson, George Math-
ews.

3

A Reluctant President

IN VIRGINIA, GEORGE WASHINGTON SUPERVISED the planting of oats, barley, and grass crops for the new growing season while he awaited official notification from New York that he had been elected president of the United States. He gave detailed instructions about how his farm was to be managed in his absence and tried to collect money that was due him, so he could pay off his debts. He even began packing for the trip north.

Early in April, Washington sent his secretary, Tobias Lear, and a black servant, Will, to New York to prepare for his arrival there. But even though the new chief executive rarely expressed his emotions, he clearly was not happy about his future. He wrote to a friend: "My movements to the chair of government will be accompanied by feelings not unlike those of a culprit who is going to the place of his execution."

At the age of fifty-seven, Washington had hoped to spend

the remaining years of his life peacefully enjoying his beloved Mount Vernon, directing agricultural experiments there. Twice before he had retired from public life—first when he gave up his position as commander in chief of the Continental Army at the end of the Revolutionary War in 1783, then after he had acted as presiding officer of the federal convention that wrote the new Constitution in 1787.

Still, Washington had a tremendous sense of duty. Even though it was his own desire to remain on his farm, he and his friends knew that he would always answer a call to serve his country.

A tall man of immense dignity, Washington had won a deeply respectful admiration among ordinary people as well as political leaders in the various states. No matter that they differed about how to solve many of the problems facing them, they all recognized that George Washington was the only man who could unify the new nation. The noted twentieth-century historian James Thomas Flexner has called him "the indispensable man." In Washington's own time, James Madison said that his leadership was the only aspect of the new government that really appealed to the majority of the people.

Yet Washington knew that the task he faced as the first president of the United States would be most difficult. Were the people of the United States capable of governing themselves? In 1789, the answer to that question was far from clear. As Americans looked abroad, they saw that all other major nations—France, England, Spain, and Russia—were ruled by kings. A federal republic, as provided for in the new Constitution, was something new on the face of the earth. Washington himself put it this way: "The preservation of the sacred fire of liberty and the destiny of the republican model of government are justly considered as deeply, perhaps as finally, staked on the experiment entrusted to the hands of the American people."

This grand experiment left the realm of theory to start becoming a reality around noon on April 14, 1789, when the springtime peace of Mount Vernon was broken by a clatter of hooves. Washington was informed that a guest had arrived. It was Charles Thomson, the agent sent by Congress, bearing a letter signed by John Langdon, presiding officer of the Senate in New York. The letter said:

> Sir, I have the honor to transmit to your Excellency the information of your unanimous election to the Office of President of the United States of America. Suffer me, Sir, to indulge the hope, that so auspicious a mark of public confidence will meet your approbation, and be considered a sure pledge of the affection and support you are to expect from a free and enlightened people.

Washington reached for a paper he had prepared and read from it:

> I am so much affected by this fresh proof of my country's esteem and confidence, that silence can best explain my gratitude—while I realize the arduous nature of the task conferred upon me, and feel my inability to perform it, I wish there may not be reason for regretting the choice. All I can promise is, only that which can be accomplished by honest zeal.

On the morning of April 16, Washington entered his carriage, accompanied by Thomson and an aide he had selected, Colonel David Humphreys, for the trip to New York. That night, the reluctant president-elect wrote in his diary, "I bade adieu to Mount Vernon, to private life, and to domestic felicity, and with a mind oppressed with more anxious and painful sensations than I have words to express, set out for New York . . . with the best disposition to render service to my country in obedience to its call, but with less hope of answering its expectations."

During the next eight days, Washington was greeted by enthusiasm and cheers in every hamlet along his route. At every stop, he had to lead a parade and make a speech. Everyone wanted to shake his hand and to wish him well. Although he began each day's journey at sunrise, it was not until April 23 that he arrived at Elizabeth Town, New Jersey, just across the Hudson River from New York City.

There the preparations dwarfed anything he had seen before. Following greetings by a committee of Congress, Washington boarded a barge manned by thirteen white-uniformed harbor pilots, one for each state of the Union, to cross the river, with an escort of numerous vessels bearing dozens of leading citizens.

Other ships fired salutes of thirteen guns as the barge carrying Washington ceremoniously moved past them. The cheering increased when he neared the landing at the foot of Wall Street and then mounted a flight of elegantly carpeted stairs prepared for his arrival. Every ship, dock, and street was crowded with people cheering and raising their hats like the rolling motion of the seas.

A parade led by elaborately garbed dragoons and grenadiers escorted Washington to his new residence. Along the way, every house displayed flags, silk banners, wreaths of flowers, and branches of evergreens. Washington, evidently moved by this outpouring of emotion, wiped tears from his eyes several times as he bowed to the crowds and took off his hat to greet the ladies in the windows of the houses he passed. They waved their handkerchiefs or threw flowers in his path. According to one observer, the streets were packed so closely that you might have walked on people's heads for a great distance.

Washington's own feelings during this demonstration of affection and emotion were described in a biography of him by one of America's first major authors, Washington Irving. He said the president had told him: "The display of boats which attended and joined us on this occasion, some with vocal and some with instrumental music on board; the decorations of the ships, the roar of cannon, and the loud acclamations of the people which rent the skies, as I passed along the wharves, filled my mind with sensations as painful (considering the reverse of the scene, which may be the case after all my labors to do good) as they are pleasing."

After Washington's effusive welcome and a dinner in his honor, he retired to a house that he had rented on Cherry Street. The house, standing "five windows wide and three stories high," had been built by a wealthy merchant in 1770 and had been previously occupied by presidents of the Continental Congress. Although the building no longer stands, its site is marked by a tablet on a pier of the Brooklyn Bridge.

New York continued in a festive mood following the arrival of Washington. Members of Congress eagerly awaited the opportunity to see him. John Adams of Massachusetts, the new vice president, had arrived a few days earlier and had taken his seat as the presiding officer of the new Senate. Both the Senate and the House of Representatives appointed committees to call upon the new president to plan the formal inaugural set for the thirtieth of April.

At sunrise that morning, a salute was fired from the guns at the Battery on the tip of Manhattan Island, opening the day's festivities. A procession formed in front of Washington's house, led by a troop of horses, then committees of

In 1797, George Holland executed this view of New York's Broad Street. The building in the background with the many columns had served as Federal Hall, and George Washington was inaugurated on its second-story balcony in 1789. *Stokes Collection; New York Public Library.*

Congress and official guests. When Washington emerged he wore clothes completely of American manufacture, as he had promised, unusual at a time when well-off Americans imported their clothes from England or France. He was dressed in a dark brown suit, made in Connecticut, with white silk stockings and black shoes adorned by silver buckles. At his side was a steel-hilted sword. His hair was powdered and tied behind in a queue, as was the custom of the era.

Washington entered his carriage, drawn by four horses, for the short trip to Federal Hall. When the head of the parade reached the building, the troops opened their ranks to form a guard of honor as the president arrived. Members of the Congress took their seats in the Senate chamber. When Washington appeared, he was received by Vice President John Adams, who informed him that all was ready for the inaugural ceremony.

Walking out onto a gallery overlooking Wall Street, Washington placed his hand on his heart and bowed to the crowd below. The cheering stopped when Chancellor Robert R. Livingston, the leading judge in New York, stepped forward to administer the oath of office set forth in the Constitution.

With his hand upon a Bible, Washington repeated: "I do solemnly swear that I will faithfully execute the office of President of the United States and will, to the best of my ability, preserve, protect and defend the Constitution of the United States." Then he bent down and kissed the Bible.

Livingston emotionally cried, "Long live the President of the United States!" Cheers rang out, church bells pealed, and artillery guns fired a noisy tribute. Washington silently bowed again to the crowd before retiring indoors to deliver his inauguration speech.

In his brief address, he mentioned his mixed emotions on becoming president—on leaving Mount Vernon to answer the call of duty and facing the unknown difficulties ahead. He repeated his promise to do the best he could. He also said he would not take any pay for the period he was president but would accept reimbursement only for his expenses.

One member of the House of Representatives set down a full account of the proceedings. "It was a very touching scene, and quite of the solemn kind," Fisher Ames recalled. "His aspect grave, almost to sadness; his modesty almost shaking; his voice deep, a little tremulous, and so low as to call for close attention." Other witnesses said that Washington's face was grave and his manner slightly awkward. As he spoke, he moved his manuscript from his left hand to his right and put his free hand into the pocket of his breeches.

When Washington finished, another procession formed to escort the president to St. Paul's Chapel for a religious service. After the service ended Washington retired to his home, where he quietly rested. But the city, ablaze with illuminations, celebrated again that night. Federal Hall was brilliantly lit, the ship *North Carolina* looked "like a pyramid of stars" in the harbor, and at the Battery a display of fireworks lasted for two hours.

The next day, after all the ceremony and celebration, the business of government began. To Washington as well as to other thoughtful citizens, it was plain that there were no precedents to follow, that new paths had to be taken in organizing the government and putting it to work. Washington himself put it this way, in a letter to James Madison: "As the first in everything, in our situation, will serve to establish a Precedent, it is devoutly wished on my part, that these precedents may be fixed on true principles."

Being a realist, Washington also knew that he had little experience in civil administration; his background was mainly in conducting military operations. Did the public that greeted him so heartily expect too much? He wrote: "I fear, if the issue of public measures should not correspond with their sanguine expectations, they will turn the extravagant and I may say undue praises which they are heaping upon me at this moment, into equally extravagant (though I will fondly hope unmerited) censures."

What happened first of all, though, resulted in neither praise nor censure, but high comedy.

4

High Comedy

A WEEK BEFORE WASHINGTON'S INAUGURATION, members of Congress began to express serious concern about what they would call the new president. Should he be His Excellency? Or perhaps His Highness? Or even His Elective Majesty? Many of the new representatives and senators thought that the title provided in the Constitution—simply, the President of the United States of America—did not sound sufficiently important for the high office.

So a joint committee of both chambers had been appointed to consider the question. After due deliberation, the committee decided: "It is not proper to annex any style or title to the respective styles or titles of office expressed in the Constitution." That should have ended the matter, but it did not. Although the House of Representatives agreed with the report, the Senate was not satisfied. For three weeks thereafter, senators sometimes heatedly debated the subject of titles.

We know the details of the debate because Senator William Maclay of Pennsylvania, a sour man who looked upon everything and everybody with suspicion, kept a daily journal of events in both the Senate and the city. That journal disappeared until 1880, when it was first published. Since then, almost every history relies on Maclay's reporting because his candid notes are the only continuous record of the early days of the Senate—when all of its sessions went on behind closed doors.

In 1789, Maclay was fifty-five years old, a lawyer and a former judge. With a home in Harrisburg, he represented the farming interests of western Pennsylvania. He was a strong opponent of many of the measures proposed by the Federalists, criticizing them with a caustic wit in his private diary. Some say that his comments were so barbed becase he suffered severely from rheumatism.

Today, it may seem comic that so much time was devoted to so trivial a question as the chief executive's title, but during the opening weeks of Washington's presidency, the issue had more than symbolic importance. Those who favored an elaborate title felt they were thereby bestowing dignity on a new office in a new government—insuring respect from the American people and from foreign governments. Opponents, though, held that the high-sounding titles smacked of monarchy and brought up the dangers of despotism against which they had recently fought a revolution.

Senator Oliver Ellsworth of Connecticut opened the debate on behalf of those favoring a more imposing style of addressing the nation's chief. "All the world, civilized and savage, called for titles," he said, insisting that there must be something in human nature bringing about such universal practice. Didn't that mean, therefore, that titles were necessary?

To this, Maclay, according to his own account, replied that

events of the past twenty years, especially the American Revolution, had diminished the widespread veneration for titles. He said that "the abuse of power and the fear of bloody masters had extorted titles as well as adoration, in some instances from the trembling crowd; that the impression now on the minds of the citizens of these States was that of horror for kingly authority."

In his journal, Maclay observed that Vice President Adams, the presiding officer of the Senate, repeatedly supported the speakers in favor of titles—even though he had a consistent record of opposition to King George III from the earliest days of the American Revolution. But Adams was a stubborn and tactless man, who had grown increasingly conceited as his career advanced. Was it possible that he looked forward to being addressed as His Excellency himself?

Yet he had started life more humbly. The son of a Massachusetts farmer, Adams had been sent to Harvard College and then became a lawyer in Boston when he was only twenty-three years old. His marriage to a minister's daughter with a very good mind of her own brought him much happiness, although he and his cherished Abigail were often separated by his increasing involvement with public business. During the Stamp Act troubles in 1765, he had written long articles for a local newspaper denouncing the British tax, which led to his election to the first Continental Congress.

Before leaving for Philadelphia in 1774, Adams had been warned by one of his friends that taking sides so openly against the British would ruin his career. Adams replied with a pithy defense of his patriotism: "Sink or swim, survive or perish, I am with my country from this day forward." So, in later years, he was often referred to as "Old Sink or Swim."

Throughout the Revolutionary War, he had served on so many committees of the Continental Congress that he was in effect the civilian secretary of war. Sometimes that had put him at odds with Washington, the commander in chief of the army, especially in dealing with requests for more arms and more money, which the Continental Congress did not have. After the war, Adams, together with Benjamin Franklin and John Jay, negotiated the 1783 treaty of peace with Britain. Following that, he was the first American minister to London, being absent from the United States when the Constitution was adopted.

Besides being ambitious and talented, Adams had the good fortune to come from the most populous of the northern states but the misfortune, in terms of political advancement, of living under the shadow of Washington, the preeminent American of the day. As long as Washington remained in public life, Adams could expect only subordinate rank. He was elected the first vice president as much because he represented Massachusetts as because of his own outstanding contributions to the nation.

Gifted as he was, Adams cherished such a high opinion of his own importance that he could not be happy as vice president. Furthermore, he and Washington did not get along well together. Washington had no intention of working intimately with him. He could have made the vice president a major figure in his administration, even his chief assistant, but he chose instead to leave Adams outside his inner circle. That left Adams with the sole function of presiding over the Senate.

Adams made no secret of his dissatisfaction, commenting caustically: "My country has in its wisdom contrived for me the most insignificant office that ever the invention of man contrived or his imagination conceived." And he brooded in private letters that "today I am nothing" even while realizing that "tomorrow I may be everything."

In that bitter state of mind, Adams plunged right into the Senate debates on the question of titles, instead of merely presiding over it. When Senator Ellsworth noted how common the word *president* was, Adams added glumly that even fire companies and cricket clubs had officials called president. When Senator Lee said he believed some states authorized the use of titles, Adams quickly said that Connecticut did.

The sour Senator Maclay could not remain silent. He read aloud the clauses in the Constitution against titles of nobility and forbidding acceptance of titles from foreign nations. He also called the attention of his fellow senators to the dangers they faced in possibly causing a break with the House of Representatives, which had rejected any title.

Despite his argument, the Senate refused to give up its quest for a proper title for President Washington. Maclay persisted, too. It was impossible, he said, to add to the respect already enjoyed by General Washington. Maclay contended that it would really be degrading the president "to place him on a par with any prince of any blood in Europe" by the use of a title, because none of them could enter "the list of true glory with him."

The Senate debate resulted in the appointment of a committee to consider a title for the president. "This whole silly business is the work of Mr. Adams and Mr. Lee," said Maclay, adding that he thought the Senate was determined on a royal court in America "to run into all the folleries, fopperies, fineries and pomp of royal etiquette, and all this for Mr. Adams."

John Adams was our nation's first vice president. Portrait by Charles Willson Peale. *Independence National Historical Park Collection*.

On the very next day, the new committee came back and recommended a truly grandiose title for the president—His Highness the President of the United States and Protector of the Rights of the Same. Then the clerk of the House of Representatives appeared before the Senate and announced that the House had adopted a report rejecting any additional titles for the president.

Despite that, several senators were not willing to let the subject drop and kept repeating their arguments over and over again. Finally, Maclay moved that a conference committee be appointed to consider the differences between the two houses of Congress, which would in effect kill the proposal, since the House opposed any title. That seemed to anger Adams, who arose and "for forty minutes did he harangue us from the chair," on the "immense advantage" and "absolute necessity" of titles, Maclay reported. He quoted the vice president as follows:

"Gentlemen, I must tell you that it is you and the president that have the making of titles. Suppose the president to have the appointment of Mr. Jefferson at the court of France. Mr. Jefferson is, in virtue of that appointment, the most illustrious, the most powerful and what not. But the president must be himself something that includes all the dignities of the diplomatic corps and something greater. What will the common people of foreign countries, what will the soldiers and sailors say, 'George Washington, President of the United States?' They will despise him to all eternity."

That argument seemed so absurd to Maclay that he rose to speak again. "Mr. President," he said, addressing Adams, the presiding officer, "the Constitution of the United States has designated our chief magistrate by the appellation of the President of the United States. That is his title of office, nor can we alter, add to, or diminish it without infringing the Constitution."

In typically bureaucratic fashion, the discussion ended with the appointment of another committee to meet with the House of Representatives. In the House, which had voted against any titles, its members indicated that they did not intend to change their minds but would, as a matter of courtesy, meet with the Senate committee. Once again, though, the representatives talked at length about the meaning of titles.

James Madison, the leading figure in the House, summed up the arguments against titles this way: "My strongest objection is founded on principle; instead of increasing, they diminish the true dignity and importance of a republic. . . . If we give titles, we must either borrow or invent them. . . . The more truly honorable shall we be, by showing a total neglect and disregard to things of this nature; the more simple, the more republican we are in our manners, the more rational dignity we shall acquire."

A joint committee did meet and each side held fast to its position. The House opposed any new title, the Senate favored one, which meant no action would be taken, because any proposal required the approval of both houses. Instead of dropping the matter, however, the Senate put on the record its position—that while it approved a new title for the president, it would conform to the practice of the House and address Washington as "the President of the United States."

So, Maclay had won. "I have by plowing with the heifer of the other House, completely defeated them," he said, referring to those who had backed elaborate titles.

Even though the battle was over, however, the arguments were not. Meeting Maclay several days later, Adams said:

"You are against titles. But there are no people in the world in favor of titles as the people of America; and the government will never be properly administered until they are adopted in the fullest manner."

To which, Maclay replied: "Instead of adding respect to government, I consider that they will bring the personages who assume them into contempt and ridicule."

But what did Washington himself feel about titles?

At the height of the debate, Washington invited Senator Maclay to sit in his box at the theater to see a performance of *The School for Scandal*. Maclay reported that he had tried to find out Washington's position but got no clue. Still the invitation and its timing were one indication of Washington's position.

In a letter to a friend, Washington gave a more precise answer about his feelings. He wrote that he "lamented" that the subject had been raised, adding, in his stilted language, that it was done "without any privity or knowledge of it on my part, and urged after I was apprized of it contrary to my opinion." He said, "Happily the matter is now done with, I hope never to be revived"—and it never was.

Ironically, the only title that came out of those long days of discussion was one of derision. Those who disliked and disagreed with Vice President Adams, who was rather short, stout, and pompous in manner, started to call him His Rotundity.

5

The Great Departments

WHILE THE NEW GOVERNMENT gradually became organized, President Washington faced many embarrassing
moments, for he had hundreds of jobs to fill—and people
kept putting themselves forward, begging to be appointed as
a postmaster, a judge, or even a clerk in one of the new
departments.

But Washington was a cautious man, not willing to make
any appointments before he considered them carefully. To
his close associates he stressed that he had made no commit-
ments to anyone and would seek the best candidate for each
vacancy, usually consulting the senators from the applicant's
state. Yet it proved difficult to carry out his resolve, because
many of the applicants were old personal friends.

No application caused him more pain than one from his
nephew, Bushrod Washington, then a twenty-seven-year-old
lawyer. Bushrod asked for the post of United States attorney
for the state of Virginia, one of the most important legal positions in the state. In reply, the president wrote: "However

deserving you may be of the [office] you have suggested, your standing at the bar would not justify my nomination of you . . . in preference to some of the oldest and most esteemed . . . lawyers in your own State, who are desirous of the appointment."

Then Washington went on to state his policy. "My political conduct in nominations, even if I was uninfluenced by principle, must be exceedingly circumspect and proof against criticism, for . . . no slip will pass unnoticed that can be improved into a supposed partiality for friends and relatives." As a result, Bushrod Washington did not get that job. Even so, it did not hinder his career; he later became a justice of the Supreme Court.

In the early months of Washington's first term, the government comprised only a handful of men. They had to cope with an empty treasury, a heavy burden of debt, and no tax system or other source of revenue. What's more, the United States had neither federal courts nor a navy, and its army consisted of just 672 officers and men. Other governmental functions were only implied in the various clauses of the Constitution. It remained for the president and Congress to organize the executive departments that would actually carry out those responsibilities.

They had a rickety framework on which to build. From the old Continental Congress, the new nation had inherited a handful of employees, anxiously waiting to see if they would keep their jobs. Prudence required that the old structure of government be maintained until a new one replaced it. So, in New York as well as in other cities throughout the thirteen states and abroad, governmental employees continued working at their jobs, even though there was no legal basis for their employment.

While waiting for Congress to establish new executive departments, Washington asked John Jay to remain as acting secretary of foreign affairs and Henry Knox as acting secretary of war. Jay had two clerks to aid him and two representatives abroad, Thomas Jefferson as minister to France and William Carmichael as chargé d'affaires in Spain. Knox had only one clerk to help him manage the army, which was largely stationed in the Northwest Territory, trying to keep peace with the Indians.

Two other agencies also remained from the Confederation. At the Treasury, thirty-nine employees, including auditors, clerks, and messengers, worked under the direction of a three-man Board of the Treasury—Samuel Osgood, William Livingston, and Arthur Lee. The Post Office Department, then an arm of the Treasury, maintained seventy-five post offices around the country, with twenty-six post riders delivering the mail to them.

Demonstrating an impressive efficiency, the new Congress in the summer of 1789 got down to the job of creating the necessary agencies. It quickly agreed that three major departments were needed in the executive branch: Foreign Affairs, War, and Treasury. Laws to create them were passed and signed by President Washington as follows: July 27—the Department of Foreign Affairs (on September 15, its name was changed to the Department of State); August 7—the War Department; and September 2—the Treasury Department.

In addition, Congress created two agencies that were considered of slightly lesser importance. On September 22, Washington signed a law that established the Post Office Department, again as a subsidiary of the Treasury Department. Two days later, on September 24, he signed another law establishing the office of Attorney General. The first holder of that post, however, would not be a full-time government employee, but only the adviser to the president on legal matters, with the right to maintain a private law practice on the side. That second law also organized the judicial system of the United States, which will be discussed in Chapter 8.

Three issues concerning power and who would exercise it arose during the debates in Congress on the mechanics of setting up the executive departments. Representative John Vining of Delaware proposed another department to supervise the records of the government, relations with the states, and other domestic matters. But his plan was rejected and most of these functions were assigned to the State Department.

A more intense dispute developed over the matter of whether the great power that would be exercised by the head of the Treasury Department was too much for one man. Such an official, it was feared, would actually exert more control over the nation's purse than Congress itself. Why not continue the existing three-man Board of the Treasury? But memories of that inefficient body under the Continental Congress proved to be strongly negative. The solution arrived at was to appoint one man secretary of the treasury, but to require him to make frequent reports directly to the House of Representatives instead of through the president.

The third controversy—about the procedure for removing presidential appointees from office—caused the most intense debate. It was clear that the Constitution assigned the Senate the power to give "advice and consent" to the president on the appointment of major federal employees. The document said nothing, however, about whether the Senate also had to give "advice and consent" before the president could dispense with the services of such an appointee. Could the president, then, exercise power on his own?

One group in Congress contended that removals as well as

appointments were subject to action by the Senate. "It is a maxim in legislation as well as reason, that it requires the same power to repeal as to enact," said Senator Maclay of Pennsylvania. But a second group insisted that the power to remove was the president's alone. Then there was a third contingent holding that, since the Constitution was silent on the matter, Congress could use its own judgment about where to place the removal power.

The debate reflected the continuing fear of some legislators that too much power in the hands of the president would lead to a monarchy. Although they agreed that Washington himself could be trusted, they worried whether future presidents might abuse the power. Others contended, however, that there could be little energy, unity, or responsibility in the executive branch if the president did not have a free hand in removing officials who proved to be either unfit or unable to conform to the president's policy.

In the House of Representatives, a clear majority recognized the right of the president to remove without Senate approval. But in the Senate, opinion split down the middle—not surprising, since the matter referred to senatorial as well as presidential powers. The vote on the issue in the Senate turned out to be a tie, ten for, ten against. The tie was broken, as provided for in the Constitution, when the Senate's presiding officer, Vice President Adams, voted to put the responsibility solely in the hands of the executive. It was a decision of prime importance, not only further defining the powers of the president but also limiting the Senate's role in the operations of the executive branch of government.

How did Washington pick the men who served as his first chief assistants? One of his own rules was that he would not appoint anyone known to be an enemy of the Constitution.

But he had three other principal criteria: Fitness for office, "former merits or sufferings in the service," and place of residence. The latter was aimed to assure a geographic balance on the roster of government officials.

In addition, Washington regularly consulted with friends, notably James Madison. Washington knew that the nation was watching carefully. "If unjudicious or unpopular measures should be taken by the Executive under the new government with regard to appointments, the government itself would be in the utmost danger of being subverted by those measures," he wrote.

Washington's first major appointment could hardly have been more important. As the nation's first secretary of the treasury, he chose a brilliant advocate of a strong central government based on sound money, a man already a major figure at the age of only thirty-four.

Alexander Hamilton, when barely in his twenties, had first distinguished himself by serving as one of Washington's aides during the Revolutionary War. After the war, he became a leading lawyer in New York and assured himself of a high social position by marrying into one of the state's most prominent families, the Schuylers.

With James Madison, he had been largely responsible for calling the convention in Philadelphia that produced the Constitution. He had worked tirelessly to win support for ratifying the Constitution, collaborating with Madison and Jay in writing *The Federalist*, a series of essays learnedly upholding the new document. Amid the swirling political currents of New York, he almost single-handedly achieved a favorable vote at the state's ratification convention.

A man of many ideas, Hamilton distrusted the mass of the people. He believed that government should be run by an elite class, which had the most to lose if peace and prosperity could not be maintained. Strongly set on acting upon his beliefs, he took over the responsibility for the new nation's finances on September 11.

On the following day, Henry Knox of Massachusetts, a genial, portly man then thirty-nine years of age, officially became the secretary of war, removing the word *acting* from his title. A bookseller in Boston, he had been an artillery officer during the Revolutionary War, rising to the rank of major general. He was a stout man, weighing nearly three hundred pounds, forceful and often profane in language, a good soldier but a poor administrator. He and his wife lived lavishly, entertaining, as one observer put it, "in the style of a prince." His wife was almost as heavy as he was, and they became known in New York as "the largest couple in the city." Although her social blunders led to much amusement, the Knoxes remained at the center of the government's social circle because they were friends of the Washingtons.

In filling the office of secretary of state, Washington thought first of John Jay of New York, the acting secretary. But Jay, whom he admired, had already expressed another preference—as we shall see in Chapter 8. So Washington turned instead to Thomas Jefferson of Virginia, then abroad in Paris as the minister to France, officially appointing him on September 26. Because of the difficulties of communication and travel, Jefferson did not take up his new duties until March 22, 1790.

Best known as the author of the Declaration of Independence, Jefferson was forty-six years old when he assumed direction of the nation's foreign affairs. He had served for five years with Washington as a member of the Virginia House of Burgesses before the Revolutionary War. During the war, he had been governor of Virginia and later a member of the Continental Congress. Although he belonged by birth to Virginia's landed aristocracy, Jefferson already had given evidence of becoming a leading spokesman for the nation's small farmers and a critic of its moneyed interests. In his view, the ideal government was the least possible government—"a few plain duties to be performed by a few servants," as he put it.

Washington made two other key appointments in those first months, selecting Edmund Randolph of Virginia as the attorney general and Samuel Osgood of New York as postmaster general. Randolph had made a name for himself at the Constitutional Convention by introducing the Virginia Plan for organizing a new government. When the Constitution was adopted, Randolph at first had opposed it but later changed his mind and urged its ratification. Osgood, who had served as a member of the Continental Congress during the Revolutionary War, was one of the three-man Board of the Treasury that directed the nation's finances until Hamilton's appointment. He and his wife, a rich widow when he had married her, owned the house in which Washington lived in New York City.

In addition to these major appointments, Washington had hundreds of minor jobs to fill. On June 15, he had made his very first nomination for an office—of William Short to take charge of affairs in Paris during Jefferson's absence. Short was promptly confirmed by the Senate. Then on August 3, Washington submitted the names of one hundred and two nominees for various offices such as collectors of customs, surveyors, and ship inspectors at ports. All of the nominees except one were confirmed.

That one was Benjamin Fishbourne, nominated as federal officer for the port of Savannah, Georgia. Fishbourne had served in the Revolutionary War from 1776 until 1783, rising to the rank of colonel, with much praise from his commanding officers. Yet Fishbourne's nomination was opposed by Georgia's senators, who preferred someone else. Washington was annoyed and wrote a letter to the Senate explaining why he had chosen Fishbourne. But in deference to the Senate's power, he later substituted another candidate.

And so Benjamin Fishbourne has gone down in the history books as a footnote—the first person to be rejected for a federal appointment—but the incident had greater significance. It was the first example of "senatorial courtesy," the practice whereby the Senate as a whole declines to approve any appointment that is opposed by the senators of the appointee's home state.

When all of the appointments had been made and the various governmental departments had begun to function, how did they operate? What role did Washington play in the daily business of the government?

From all accounts, Washington was a skillful administrator. He himself made all the major decisions and many minor ones. Today he would be counted among those top officials whose hands-on style distinguishes them from those who prefer to delegate many tasks to their subordinates. In Washington's administration, no department head settled any matter of importance without consulting the president and obtaining his approval. But while Washington made the final decisions, he usually did so only after consulting his department heads and other advisers, often in writing and sometimes in person.

Of course, the nation was small then, which made it comparatively easy for Washington to keep in touch with everyone in the executive department. In those simpler days, government was highly personal, both at the presidential level and within the departments of government. For example, Congress voted lump-sum appropriations for the various departments, leaving it to the individual department heads to decide how to spend the money. However, Washington himself decided how much to pay American ministers abroad.

As his office aides, Washington had two secretaries at first—Tobias Lear and Colonel David Humphreys, who had been with him at Mount Vernon before his election. As the workload grew, he added another principal secretary, Major William Jackson, who had served as secretary of the Constitutional Convention. For policy and political advice, Washington generally turned to James Madison, John Jay, and Alexander Hamilton.

From the beginning, it was Washington's practice to ask his department heads to their opinions in writing. He kept them busy, referring to them proposed plans of action, drafts of his public papers, and answers to the numerous letters for help that he received. Often, after receiving an answer, he would ask a department head to breakfast to discuss a problem until he was satisfied with the answer.

The system worked this way, according to a description by Jefferson:

> Letters of business came frequently addressed sometimes to the President, but most frequently to the heads of the departments. If addressed to himself, he referred them to the proper department to be acted on; if to one of the secretaries, the letter, if it required no answer, was communicated to the President for his information.

> If an answer was requisite, the secretary of the department communicated the letter and his proposed answer to the President. Generally, they were sent back after perusal, which signified his approbation. Sometimes he returned them with an informal note, suggesting an alteration or a query. If a doubt of any importance arose, he reserved it for conference.

By this means, he was always in accurate possession of all facts and proceedings in every part of the Union, and to whatsoever department they related; he formed a central point for the different branches; preserved a unity of object and action among them; exercised that participation in the suggestion of affairs incumbent on him; and met himself the due responsibility for whatever was done.

[His system] gave, indeed, to the heads of the departments the trouble of making up, once a day, a packet of all their communications for the perusal of the President; it commonly also retarded one day the dispatches by mail. But in pressing cases, this injury was prevented by presenting that case singly for immediate attention; and it produced in return the benefit of his sanction for every act we did.

Washington accepted full responsibility for all actions by the federal government, never saying he did not know what was going on or putting the blame on a subordinate. Throughout the eight years of his presidency, there is no indication that he considered his department heads as other than assistants to the president.

In the affairs of the War Department, Washington was an expert, the preeminent military man of his day. In foreign affairs, Washington also considered himself to be knowledgeable, and so kept a firm hand in dealing with other nations. But he was less interested in finance and commerce, and so Hamilton as secretary of the treasury had a freer hand in those matters than Jefferson and Knox had in their departments, as we shall see in a later chapter.

6

Social Life

UNFORTUNATELY, GEORGE WASHINGTON HAD ENDURED painful troubles with his teeth for many years. At the age of only twenty-one, he had lost his first tooth, and that unhappy experience kept being repeated. By the time he came to New York as president, he already was using false teeth that did not fit properly. The discomfort they caused may have been the reason he rarely smiled or laughed. But in New York he finally found a good dentist—John Greenwood, the city's leading practitioner.

At that time, dentistry was in its infancy. In Boston, Greenwood's father practiced dentistry on the side, but his main business was making mathematical instruments. John Greenwood himself had been apprenticed as a cabinetmaker before the Revolutionary War. But after brief service in the army and at sea, he earned enough money making furniture to be able to study dental mechanics. In 1784, he set up an office in New York and soon became an expert at making false teeth.

Greenwood used spiral springs to hold artificial teeth in place. Sometimes he carved artificial teeth out of ivory. He even bought teeth from poor people, who sold their good teeth for cash, to use in his dentures. This ingenious dentist used beeswax to make casts of Washington's jaws. Then he carved dental plates from hippopotamus tusk, attaching human teeth to the plates with gold wire. Washington was so pleased with his new false teeth that he would go to no other dentist for the rest of his life.

It was a good thing that Washington solved this problem soon after his arrival in New York, because he found himself caught up not only in the complications of establishing a new government but also in the social life of the new capital. Besides his basic task of trying to define his own role, he had to study foreign dispatches and treasury reports, confer with heads of departments, establish good relations with members of Congress, consider appointments to office, and organize the executive department of the government. How could he do all this if, in addition, he had to receive visitors, attend dinners and receptions, and make appearances at civic functions?

In his characteristic way, Washington sought the advice of such associates as John Adams, John Jay, James Madison, and Alexander Hamilton before working out a schedule for his official entertaining. He decided to hold receptions on Tuesdays from three to four in the afternoon for men only. His wife would give tea parties for men and women on Friday evenings. And they both would be hosts at official dinners on Thursdays at four in the afternoon.

Washington decided, too, that he would devote at least some of his time to things he enjoyed—such as going to the theater on occasion and visiting nearby farms. But he left numerous other decisions on social life to await the arrival of his wife, who was still in Virginia. Meanwhile, he would make no visits to private homes or parties.

On May 1, the day after his inauguration, Washington received visits from Vice President John Adams, Governor George Clinton of New York, the heads of various governmental departments, and other distinguished persons. On May 6, he made his first public appearance, at the commencement exercises of Columbia College. On the following night, he attended a ball at the Assembly Room, on the east side of Broadway near Wall Street, which has come to be known as the first inaugural ball, with both ladies and gentlemen dressed in the height of fashion.

According to a writer of the time: "Surveying the assemblage, President Washington naturally exercised his prerogative, as he always did, and chose the prettiest of the women to dance with." He danced with Mrs. Peter Van Brugh Livingston, Elizabeth Schuyler Hamilton, the wife of Alexander Hamilton, and a Miss Van Zandt. He had such a good time that he did not leave until two o'clock in the morning, a very late hour for him.

A few days later, on May 11, he invited several senators and other officials to share his box at the John Street Theatre for a performance of *The School for Scandal*. Washington loved the theater and attended often. But one of the senators, the cranky William Maclay of Pennsylvania, was not amused. "I am old and notices and attentions are lost on me," he wrote in his diary. "I could have wished some of my dear children in my place; they are young and would have enjoyed it. Long might they boast of having been seated in the same box as the first Character in the world."

Washington did not appear to relish his receptions for men, though. These hour-long gatherings, called levees after the French fashion, were open without invitation to any respectably dressed man. In keeping with the formal tone of the era's entertaining, however, it was accepted that only men from the upper ranks of society would attend. "We had a numerous and splendid circle," said Washington's secretary, Tobias Lear, after the first levee. But there was an embarrassing moment for Washington soon after.

On that occasion, David Humphreys, one of his aides, waited for the guests to gather in the reception room. Then, throwing open the door to the room, he announced in a loud voice, "The President of the United States." Washington was annoyed and angry at what he considered to be excessive homage. When the reception was over, he told his aide, "Well, you have taken me in once, but by God, you will never take me in a second time."

Thereafter at his receptions, Washington stood in front of the fireplace, facing the door, wearing his most formal attire—a suit of black velvet, a long sword at his left hip in a scabbard of white leather, and stylish yellow gloves on his hands. Under one arm, he held a cocked hat. His hair was powdered white and gathered behind him. According to one account:

> He received his visitor with a dignified bow, while hands were so disposed of as to indicate that the salutation was not to be accompanied with shaking hands. This ceremony never occurred in these visits, even with his most near friends that no distinction might be made.
>
> As visitors came in, they formed a circle around the room. At a quarter past three, the door was closed, and the circle was formed for that day. He then began on the right, and spoke to each visitor, calling him by name, and exchanging a few words with him. When he completed his circuit, he re-

sumed his first position and the visitors approached him in succession, bowed and retired. By four o'clock, this ceremony was over.

When Martha Washington, accompanied by her grandchildren, arrived in New York in late May, the social life of the capital bustled even more. Her old friends, the wives of public officials, and those who were socially prominent did not require an invitation to attend her parties, as was the custom of the times, but Mrs. Washington did invite some others. Every woman wore formal dress for those occasions, with elaborate hairstyles and gowns.

Washington, who liked the company of women, was much more at ease at his wife's tea parties than at his own receptions. Mrs. Washington remained seated, but the president moved around, chatting with the women. Washington was careful to see that Abigail Adams, the vice president's wife, sat on Mrs. Washington's right. If another woman happened to be sitting there when Mrs. Adams arrived, Washington tactfully led the misplaced guest somewhere else. One biographer has said that he made special efforts to observe this protocol because he really didn't like this lady's husband and did not get on well with him.

Abigail Adams, herself one of the most acute observers of her time, described Washington this way: "This same President has so happy a faculty of appearing to accommodate and yet carrying his point, that, if he was not really one of the best-intentioned men in the world, he might be a very dangerous man." She also said, "He is polite with dignity, affable without familiarity, distant without haughtiness, grave without austerity, modest, wise and good."

Someone else who attended Mrs. Washington's very first tea party told this anecdote: "Amid the social chit-chat of the company, the hall clock struck nine. Mrs. Washington thereupon rose with dignity, and, looking around the company with a complacent smile, observed, 'The General always retires at nine, and I usually precede him.' At this hint, the ladies instantly arose, adjusted their dresses, made their salutations and retired."

At formal dinners, Mrs. Washington sat at one side of the table, flanked by the other women, while Washington sat opposite her, with the other men. The meals were elaborate. A guest at one of those dinners said that soup was followed by fish, roasted and boiled meats, and fowl. "The dessert was first apple pies, pudding etc., then iced creams, jellies,

Martha Washington enlivened the capital's social life with her skills as a hostess. Daniel Huntington (1816–1906), *The Republican Court* (also known as "Lady Washington's Reception"). *Oil on canvas, 167.6 by 277.0 cm. (66 by 109 in.), The Brooklyn Museum, 39.536.1, gift of the Crescent-Hamilton Athletic Club.*

etc., then watermelons, muskmelons, apples, peaches and nuts," Senator Maclay wrote in his diary.

After the meal was completed, President Washington proposed a toast to every individual by name around the table. The guests in turn proposed toasts, and, Senator Maclay continued, "such a buzz of 'health, sir' and 'health, madame,' never had I heard before." When the ladies withdrew to another room, leaving the men at the table, as was the custom, Washington told an anecdote about a New England clergyman who had lost a hat and a wig while crossing a river "called the Brunks," which Maclay did not find funny.

Clearly, though, Washington ate well. Dinners were large, frequent, and elaborate. Orders for wine ran to twenty-six dozen bottles at a time and food was consumed in amazing quantities. Keeping track of the purchases and preparation of the food and wine fell to the steward, Samuel Fraunces, who had operated Fraunces Tavern, where Washington had said farewell to his fellow officers of the Revolutionary War back in 1783. Every morning Fraunces went to market to buy the day's food for the Washingtons' table.

One day, according to an anecdote told about the Washington household, Fraunces bought one of the first shad of the season and prepared it for the president's breakfast.

"What is that, Sam?" asked Washington.

"Why, sir, it is a shad," replied Fraunces.

"It is early in the season for shad. How much did you pay for it?"

"Two dollars."

"Two dollars," Washington cried out angrily. "I can never encourage such extravagance at my table. Take it away. I will never touch it."

Fraunces took it out of the room and, later, ate it himself. For the women of New York, the teas and dinners with the president and his wife were major social events. But for Martha Washington, they were boring. She wrote to a friend: "I lead a very dull life here and know nothing that passes in town. I never go to any public place—indeed I think I am more like a state prisoner than anything else, there is certain bounds set for me which I must not depart from—and as I cannot do as I like I am obstinate and stay at home a great deal."

The new administration's social season came to a sudden and abrupt halt in June when the president, who had not been feeling well, was sent to bed with a serious illness. Dr. Samuel Bard, a leading physician in the city, was summoned. Washington had a high temperature caused by a large and painful swelling on his left thigh. The swelling developed into an abscess, which required an operation, a dangerous procedure in those days.

Before the operation started, Washington asked Dr. Bard's opinion of his chances. "Do not flatter me with vain hopes," he said. "I am not afraid to die, and therefore can bear the worst."

Dr. Bard replied that the outlook was hopeful, but that nothing was certain.

"Whether tonight or twenty years hence makes no difference," Washington said. "I know that I am in the hands of a good Providence."

The operation was successful and Washington began to recover slowly, lying mostly on his right side for six weeks. In that time, he did get up on occasion to ride in his carriage, its seats elongated so that he could stretch out at full length while driving around the city with his wife. By July 4, Washington was well enough to receive a delegation from the Society of the Cincinnati, composed of officers who had served under him in the Revolutionary War. On that day, he also signed a bill to collect a tax on "goods, wares and merchandizes imported into the United States."

A great believer in exercise, Washington was impatient to get out again. As he recovered, he took walks near his home or rode his horse around town. An expert rider, he kept twelve to sixteen horses in his stable. He usually rode a white horse, its saddle of leopard skin fringed with a gold binding. Six cream-colored horses pulled his carriage. Enjoying fine living, he did not feel that this kind of display was excessive. Nor did other people, for there was very little criticism of his style of living.

Following his recovery, and after the adjournment of Congress in September, Washington left on a trip through New England, traveling in a coach pulled by four bay-colored horses, with two secretaries, Tobias Lear and Major Jackson, riding alongside. Behind the carriage came a light baggage wagon, carrying his clothes, and at the rear one of his servants rode Washington's favorite white horse to be used in ceremonies along the way. For Washington, it was a combined business and pleasure trip because he aimed to become better acquainted with the people of the region as well as to enjoy a vacation. As always, he carefully noted the farming practices of each area he passed through.

When Washington reached Hartford, in Connecticut, he inspected a wool manufacturing plant, where he ordered a suit for himself and cloth for breeches for his servants. In Beverly, Massachusetts, he visited New England's first cotton mill. At Kittery, Maine, he went fishing. "It not being the proper time of tide, we only caught two," he wrote in his journal.

It was in Boston that a matter of protocol became important. Washington rode into the city on his white horse, accompanied by Vice President Adams, members of Congress, distinguished citizens, and representatives of at least forty local societies, many with banners, forming a parade that Washington called "in every degree flattering and honorable." The cannon on Dorchester Heights roared a salute and church bells rang out a welcome.

Washington wrote in his diary: "We passed through the citizens classed in their different professions and under their own banners, till we came to the State House, from which across the street an arch was thrown, in front of which was this inscription, 'To the man who unites all hearts' and on another—'To Columbia's favorite Son' . . . The procession being over, I was conducted to my lodgings at the Widow Ingersoll's (which is a very decent and honest house)."

But a problem arose. When Governor John Hancock did not call upon him at the Widow Ingersoll's to pay his respects, claiming that an attack of gout prevented him from venturing out, Washington canceled a dinner engagement at the governor's home. He dined with John Adams instead. "By this action," one historian has written, "Washington asserted the official precedence of the President of the United States over the governor of a state, the only possible rival for such precedence in the whole governmental system of the country."

Washington knew exactly what he was doing. He sent a note to Hancock: "The President of the United States presents his best respects to the Governor and has the honor to inform him that he shall be at home until 2 o'clock. The President of the United States need not express the pleasure it will give him to see the Governor, but at the same time, he most earnestly begs that the Governor will not hazard his health on the occasion."

Hancock got the message. He was carried into Washington's presence later that day by aides, with bandages on his

gouty foot. But Hancock's face-saving device only empha-
sized the triumph of Washington in this battle for official
precedence. Since then, there has never been any doubt
that the president of the United States is the first citizen of
the republic.

Washington returned to New York on November 13 and
resumed his schedule of official and social duties. Besides
attending the theater, he went out almost every day, either
on horseback or in a carriage with his wife and her two
grandchildren. One expedition took him to Baron de
Poellnitz's farm, located in what is now Manhattan's Murray
Hill neighborhood, to see a new threshing machine in operation. The President and his wife also kept dutifully giving
their teas and dinner parties.

By this time, though, the Washingtons had concluded that
their house on Cherry Street was not adequate to maintain
the dignity of the presidency. So they leased the mansion of
Alexander Macomb at 39–41 Broadway, one of the largest
residences in the city, recently occupied by the French minister. From the rear of the main rooms, glass doors opened
upon a balcony with a view of the Hudson River. On each
side of the central hallway were spacious high-ceilinged
rooms suitable for formal receptions and dinners.

Washington moved into his new home the day after his
fifty-eighth birthday, February 23, 1790. He and his wife
lived there until the government moved to Philadelphia later
that year.

7

The Bill of Rights

SEPTEMBER 24, 1789, IS A DAY TO REMEMBER. The Supreme
Court along with the entire federal judicial system came to
life on that day, and President Washington appointed John
Jay as the first chief justice of the United States, as we shall
see in the next chapter. But another momentous action
taken that same date deserves attention first—agreement by
the Senate and the House of Representatives on a bill of
rights to be added to the Constitution.

Today, almost everybody considers the Bill of Rights to be
the heart of the Constitution, yet it was not actually part of
the original document. At the Constitutional Convention in
Philadelphia in 1787, the question of including a bill of rights
had not arisen until the work of the convention was almost
over. It was George Mason, a distinguished lawyer from Virginia and the author of the bill of rights in that state's constitution, who brought up the issue.

He suggested that the proposed new Constitution be pref-
aced by a bill of rights because that would give "great quiet

to the people." Doing so would be easy, he went on, because many state constitutions already had bills of rights that
could be adapted. Elbridge Gerry of Massachusetts made a
motion to draft a bill of rights, seconded by Mason.

While it may seem incredible two hundred years later, the
motion ran into a storm of opposition—not because anyone
was against a bill of rights, but because the other delegates
thought no such addition was necessary. They looked upon
the entire Constitution as a bill of rights, with all of its provisions serving to protect the people.

Alexander Hamilton of New York demanded, Why should
the Constitution list the things that Congress could not do
after it had specifically listed what Congress could do? John
Dickinson of Pennsylvania said that trial by jury and other
specific rights must be preserved by "soundness of sense and
honesty of heart." Roger Sherman of Connecticut spoke up
dryly: "No Bill of Rights ever yet bound the supreme power
longer than the honeymoon of a newly-married couple."

So the motion to add a bill of rights was rejected unanimously, with ten states voting against it and none for it.
Even Virginia, Mason's home state, joined the opposition.
Because of that negative vote, Mason and Gerry both left
the convention, refusing to sign the Constitution.

The failure to add a bill of rights to the Constitution
turned out to be the major mistake of the convention. It
became a rallying point for the opponents of the Constitution
at state ratifying conventions, giving them a persuasive argument against it. In state after state—in Massachusetts,
South Carolina, New Hampshire, New York, and Virginia—
the pro-Constitution forces were able to win ratification only
after promising that they would introduce a bill of rights
amending the Constitution as soon as possible.

In his inaugural address, Washington called upon Congress to move swiftly to carry out the promises. He asked for constitutional amendments showing "a reverence for the characteristic rights of freemen and a regard for public harmony"—in short, a bill of rights. Soon thereafter, on June 8, 1789, James Madison, "the father of the Constitution," now a representative in Congress, arose on the floor of the House and moved that it take up the matter of constitutional amendments immediately.

Madison himself proposed nine amendments changing, and adding to, words already in the Constitution, all designed to protect individual liberties against encroachment by the federal government. The first of these proposed amendments suggested a new preamble to the Constitution, citing rights mentioned in the Declaration of Independence, that would read:

> That all power is originally vested in, and consequently derived from the people,

> That government is instituted, and ought to be exercised for the benefit of the people; which consists in the enjoyment of life and liberty; with the right of acquiring and using property, and generally of pursuing and obtaining happiness and safety.

> That the people have an indubitable, unalienable and indefeasible right to reform or change their government whenever it be found adverse or inadequate to the purposes of its institution.

When the House of Representatives began considering Madison's proposal, it made a major decision about the way the new wording would be added, creating a real bill of rights. Instead of following Madison's plan to insert the changes into the Constitution directly, the House adopted them in the form of seventeen amendments to follow the original document. When the Senate considered the proposed changes, it reduced them to twelve by combining some of them.

To settle the differences between the two chambers, a conference committee was appointed, with Madison the head of the House group and Oliver Ellsworth leading the Senate members. They quickly settled their minor differences, and on September 24 reported back to both chambers. On that day, the House accepted the Bill of Rights consisting of twelve amendments, and the Senate did so the next day.

But that did not mean that the Bill of Rights instantly became part of the Constitution. Under its Article V, three-quarters of the states must ratify any amendment either by a vote of their state legislatures or by conventions called for that purpose. When Congress passed the first amendments, the Union consisted of eleven states. With the admission of North Carolina, Rhode Island, and Vermont during the ratification period, the nation grew to fourteen states—so the affirmative vote of eleven states was needed to ratify the proposed amendments.

New Jersey became the first state to act, giving its approval on November 20, 1789. But it took more than two years until the process was completed. On December 15, 1791, Virginia became the eleventh state to ratify the Bill of Rights, thus making it part of the Constitution.

Along the way, though, only ten of the proposed amendments were approved. Many states rejected the first two of the twelve as unnecessary. One would have regulated the number of representatives in Congress and the other would have prohibited pay raises for members of Congress during their terms of office.

With Virginia's ratification, the amendments originally

proposed as the third to the twelfth became the first ten amendments to the Constitution—the Bill of Rights that we know today. To most Americans, their familiar phrases contain the essence of the Constitution—freedom of speech, freedom of religion, freedom of the press, protection against unreasonable search and seizure, the right to a trial by jury, and the right to due process of law. The actual words are well worth repeating:

AMENDMENT I

Congress shall make no law respecting an establishment of religion, or prohibiting the free exercise thereof; or abridging the freedom of speech, or of the press, or the right of the people peaceably to assemble, and to petition the Government for a redress of grievances.

AMENDMENT II

A well regulated Militia, being necessary to the security of a free State, the right of the people to keep and bear Arms shall not be infringed.

AMENDMENT III

No Soldier shall, in time of peace, be quartered in any house, without the consent of the Owner, nor in time of war, but in a manner to be prescribed by law.

AMENDMENT IV

The right of the people to be secure in their persons, houses, papers, and effects, against unreasonable searches and seizures, shall not be violated, and no Warrants shall issue, but upon probable cause, supported by Oath or affirmation, and particularly describing the place to be searched, and the persons or things to be seized.

AMENDMENT V

No person shall be held to answer for a capital or otherwise infamous crime, unless on a presentment or indictment of a Grand Jury, except in cases arising in the land or naval forces, or in the Militia, when in actual service in time of War or public danger; nor shall any person be subject for the same offence to be twice put in jeopardy of life or limb; nor shall be compelled in any criminal case to be a witness against himself, nor be deprived of life, liberty, or property, without due process of law; nor shall private property be taken for public use without just compensation.

AMENDMENT VI

In all criminal prosecutions, the accused shall enjoy the right to a speedy and public trial, by an impartial jury of the State and district wherein the crime shall have been committed, which district shall have been previously ascertained by law, and to be informed of the nature and cause of the accusation; to be confronted with the witnesses against him; to have compulsory process for obtaining witnesses in his favor, and to have the Assistance of Counsel for his defence.

AMENDMENT VII

In suits at common law, where the value in controversy shall exceed twenty dollars, the right of trial by jury shall be preserved, and no fact tried by a jury shall be otherwise reexamined in any Court of the United States, than according to the rules of the common law.

AMENDMENT VIII

Excessive bail shall not be required, nor excessive fines imposed, nor cruel and unusual punishments inflicted.

AMENDMENT IX

The enumeration in the Constitution of certain rights shall not be construed to deny or disparage others retained by the people.

AMENDMENT X

The powers not delegated to the United States by the Constitution, nor prohibited by it to the States, are reserved to the States respectively, or to the people.

As we have seen, the Bill of Rights became part of the Constitution on December 15, 1791, when Virginia ratified it. It was not until March 1, 1792, however, that Thomas Jefferson, the secretary of state, officially notified all the states that the Bill of Rights had been ratified and was part of the Constitution. And it was not until 1939, when the sesquicentennial of the Constitution was observed, that the three states that had originally failed to ratify the Bill of Rights—Massachusetts, Connecticut, and Georgia—finally did so.

8

Three Forgotten Americans

IN ORGANIZING THE NEW AMERICAN GOVERNMENT, the last great constitutional task of the first Congress was to create its judicial system. That important work was accomplished mainly by a man unknown to most Americans today—Oliver Ellsworth of Connecticut. Just as James Madison quickly emerged as the leader of the House of Representatives, Ellsworth became the leader of the Senate because of his diligence, hard work, and support of the policies of the Washington administration. Almost everything the first Senate did bore the handiwork of Oliver Ellsworth.

He came to the Senate with an outstanding record of previous service as a judge, a member of the Continental Congress, and a delegate to the Constitutional Convention, but little is known about his early life. Born in Windsor, Connecticut, in 1745, he entered Yale College in 1762 to prepare for the ministry. Two years later he was dismissed from the college, but there are no records indicating why. Whatever the reason for his dismissal, it left no hard feelings. He sent his sons to Yale, and he himself later received an honorary degree from the college.

Ellsworth graduated from Princeton and started to study theology but within a year gave that up in favor of the law. Admitted to the bar in 1771, he found his new profession in Windsor a hard way to earn a living. He had so few clients that he had to farm and chop wood to support himself and his new wife. During his first years as a lawyer, he earned only three pounds, a very small amount of money. He was so poor that he could not afford to keep a horse, and so, when he had a case in Hartford, he had to walk ten miles to the court there and ten miles home.

Ellsworth's fortunes changed when he moved to Hartford. By 1779, according to Noah Webster, who studied law under him, he had more than a thousand clients. Obviously, he prospered financially. He also became active as a state's attorney, a member of the Governor's Council, and a judge. During the Revolutionary War, he served for six years in the Continental Congress in Philadelphia.

After the war, Ellsworth joined Roger Sherman and William S. Johnson as Connecticut's representatives to the Constitutional Convention in 1787. There he collaborated with Sherman in proposing and supporting the "great compromise" on apportioning state representation in the houses of Congress that made the Constitution possible. It was Ellsworth who first suggested using the words *the United States* instead of *national* in resolutions under consideration at the convention, thereby giving the nation its name.

Elected a member of the first Senate in 1789, Ellsworth felt very much at home because he was ideally suited for the detailed work of that deliberative body. According to one colleague, he was "all powerful and eloquent in debate"— but he talked so much that Senator Maclay called him "endless Ellsworth." Although Ellsworth was a dignified man, he had the peculiar habit of talking to himself, even when other people were around. His one vice was sniffing tobacco, dropping quantities of it around him as he raised it to his nose. His family sometimes judged the intensity of his concentration by the number of piles of snuff around his chair.

Despite those peculiarities, Ellsworth's capacity for solid work brought him increasing distinction. On April 7, 1789, when the Senate opened without rules to guide it, Ellsworth was named chairman of its first two committees, one to prepare its rules of procedure and the other to establish a federal judiciary. Owing to his tireless zeal, he served on more committees than any other senator.

Although Ellsworth later rose to be a chief justice of the United States, his greatest legacy to the nation was the law he wrote that created the federal court system, including the Supreme Court. That law is still the foundation of our court system today. One historian, Forrest MacDonald, has called it "for all practical purposes, a part of the Constitution itself."

Of course, Ellsworth was not solely responsible for the Judiciary Act of 1789. He was assisted by two other senators, William Paterson of New Jersey, who had served as a judge in his home state, and Caleb Strong of Massachusetts, a former county attorney as well as a lawyer. But most authorities agree that the Judiciary Act was drafted largely by Ellsworth. Senator Maclay of Pennsylvania, who opposed portions of it, noted in his diary: "This vile bill is a child of his, and he defends it with the care of a parent."

Under the terms of the Judiciary Act, three tiers of federal courts were established. At the top was a Supreme Court of six justices (later expanded to nine). At the bottom was a district court for each of the eleven states then in the Union plus two additional district courts, one each for Virginia and Massachusetts, covering their areas that later became the states of Kentucky and Maine. In between were three circuit courts to consist of two Supreme Court justices and a local district judge, sitting together.

President Washington did not hesitate about appointing the first chief justice of the United States, which is the formal title of the Supreme Court's leader. Even before his inauguration, Washington had written to his old friend, John Jay of New York: "Whatever office you wish is yours." At that time, Jay was secretary of foreign affairs under the old Continental Congress. When Jay said he would like to be the nation's top judge, Washington felt both pleased and relieved.

Jay, despite the number of high positions he filled and the high regard of his colleagues, is another largely forgotten man in American history—at least in part because he tried hard to seem above ordinary human failings. Indeed, he thought the ideal statesman should show no more emotion than a marble statue. But his austere personality, along with his preference for the life of a gentleman farmer, did not prevent George Washington from appreciating his exceptional abilities.

It was Jay's strong sense of duty that had done most to win Washington's friendship. Jay owed this sense of duty to the stern training of his father, who had retired from a prosperous mercantile business in New York City to supervise the boy's upbringing on a country estate overlooking Long Island Sound. In 1765, at the age of only nineteen, young Jay had graduated from Kings College down in the city, and then studied law. Tall and slender, with the poised manner that came from being sure that he belonged to the top rank of New York society, Jay was elected as one of the colony's

John Jay served the new republic first as secretary for foreign affairs and then as the first chief justice. Lithograph by H.B. Hall.

delegates to the first Continental Congress—and there he first met George Washington. Of similar disposition and interests, they got along well together. Jay left the second Continental Congress to return to New York, where he played a major role in writing the first constitution for the State of New York. In 1777, when that constitution went into effect, Jay, at the young age of thirty-two, was appointed the first chief justice of the state.

Sent back to Philadelphia again, Jay was elected president of the Continental Congress during the Revolutionary War. In that post, he cemented his close personal relationship with Washington, then in the field as commander in chief of the Continental Army. Jay, hearing about a plot to remove Washington from his command, immediately wrote to him describing it. Forewarned, Washington took steps to eliminate the threat, writing Jay a sixteen-page letter expressing his thanks and reflections on politics.

During the war, Jay was sent abroad to help raise money for the struggling new nation. When the fighting ended, Jay, together with Benjamin Franklin and John Adams, negotiated the treaty of peace that recognized the independence of the new United States. On his return home, he found that the Continental Congress had appointed him secretary for foreign affairs.

He and his wife, Sally—born Sarah Livingston, the daughter of New Jersey's first governor—built a fine new home on Broadway, not far from Wall Street. There Sally Jay established herself as a distinguished hostess, presiding over elaborate banquets. Every important visitor to New York, foreign dignitaries as well as officials from other states, dined with the Jays. Meanwhile, Jay himself conducted the foreign affairs of the United States from a cramped office in Fraunces Tavern, assisted by one secretary, part-time translators, two clerks, and a doorkeeper-messenger. When the new Constitution for the United States was adopted in Philadelphia in 1787, Jay joined with Alexander Hamilton and James Madison in writing *The Federalist,* giving solid arguments why the Constitution should be ratified.

Following Washington's inauguration, he summoned Jay frequently to his house on Cherry Street to talk about governmental problems. The two men fully agreed that the establishment of a sound court system was essential for the preservation of the Constitution and the new republic. It suited them both that Jay gave up his foreign affairs post to become the first chief justice.

In naming the associate justices of the Supreme Court to serve with Jay, Washington paid careful attention to geography as well as to legal ability and a record of firm support for the Constitution. He appointed John Rutledge of South Carolina, James Iredell of North Carolina, John Blair of Virginia, James Wilson of Pennsylvania, and William Cushing of Massachusetts, all with respectable records of public service.

In those more leisurely times, the new Supreme Court justices did not take their offices immediately. Washington asked Jay to continue as secretary of foreign affairs until Thomas Jefferson returned from Paris to replace him. It was not until February 1, 1790, that the Supreme Court held its first session, in the old Royal Exchange Building in New York City. Almost immediately, though, it adjourned until the next day for lack of a quorum. The court began its real business on February 2.

Jay made a major decision that day. He held that members of the Supreme Court would wear robes of black and scarlet to enhance their dignity, but ruled against another sort of formality dating back to British times. On the bench in Massachusetts, Justice William Cushing had worn an elaborately curled white wig such as English judges wore, so he appeared this way at the new court's first session. One story is that the hooting of small boys on the street when they saw Justice Cushing walking to the Court convinced Jay and the other justices to follow the advice of Thomas Jefferson, who had said, "For heaven's sake, discard the monstrous wig which makes English judges look like rats peeping through bunches of oakum."

During Jay's tenure as chief justice, the Supreme Court differed vastly from the imposing institution that it is today. For one thing, it had no home. It did not have a building of its own until 1935, in its one hundred forty-sixth year of existence. In all those years, it met in chambers borrowed from the Congress. During those early years, very few issues came before the Supreme Court because of the time required for cases to work their way through the lower courts until they could be heard on appeal by the highest court. Its first cases reached the Supreme Court in its second year of existence, and the Court did not hand down its first formal written opinion until 1792, its third year.

Most of the work of the new Supreme Court justices was done in their capacity as circuit court judges, traveling around the nation to sit in various cities. That travel, as it turned out, was far more difficult than hearing arguments and making decisions. Because the circuit courts were held twice a year, the new Supreme Court justices had to spend many months away from their homes.

In April 1790, Chief Justice Jay rode out of New York City on horseback to convene the first session of the circuit court covering New York and New England. The weather was bad and the roads mucky. A week after his departure, he found himself marooned in Hartford by a snowstorm. All of the Supreme Court justices faced hazards such as runaway horses, overturned carriages, and icebound rivers as well as flea-ridden beds and indigestible stew in the scruffy taverns where they were often obliged to spend the night while making their rounds.

But there were compensations for Jay and the other justices. Everywhere they went, they were welcomed warmly. Chief Justice Jay, particularly, received many honors during his travels, including an honorary degree of doctor of laws from Harvard College. Although he was frequently invited to stay in the comfortable homes of friends along his route, he always declined, because he considered the acceptance of private hospitality unwise in the performance of his official duties.

Chief Justice Jay did other things, however, that would be considered improper today. He not only served as an adviser to President Washington on controversial issues, but he took an active part in politics without resigning from the bench. In 1792, while sitting as chief justice, he ran for governor of New York against George Clinton, the Anti-Federalist incumbent. Jay got more votes than his opponent, but the Clintonians, who controlled the state legislature, refused to count the ballots of three counties on a technicality, thus giving the election to Clinton.

Jay accepted that decision. He said, "A few years more will put us all in the dust, and it will then be of more importance to me to have governed myself, than to have governed New York." He immersed himself in the work of the Supreme Court.

The Court's first really important case, that of *Chisholm* v. *Georgia*, came up in 1793. The issue was simple: Could a state be sued against its wishes in the nation's highest court? The case arose when two residents of South Carolina tried to collect a debt from the estate of a resident of Georgia, only to find out that the property of the deceased, a Tory during the Revolutionary War, had been confiscated by the state of Georgia.

Looking back, we are bound to find it extraordinary that the lawyer for Chisholm was Edmund Randolph, the attorney general of the United States, arguing in the Supreme Court for a private client. At that time, though, the attorney general occupied a unique position. Even though he attended cabinet meetings and served as the legal adviser to the president, he was only a part-time employee, with an annual retainer of $1,500 a year, half the pay received by other department heads. Randolph was not only allowed but expected to continue his legal work for private clients while also representing the federal government.

Randolph complained about his peculiar position in a letter to a friend: "I am sort of a mongrel between the State and the U.S.; called an officer of some rank under the latter, and yet thrust out to get a livelihood in the former—perhaps in a petty mayor's or county court."

Like Jay and Ellsworth, Edmund Randolph has been almost forgotten today, although he played an important if secondary role in the first days of the United States. Born into one of the first families of Virginia in 1753, he made his mark at an early age. After studying law, he became an aide to General Washington in 1775, when he was only twenty-two. A year later, he returned to Williamsburg to serve as the youngest member of the Virginia convention that adopted the first constitution for that state. He also became the attorney general of the state and the mayor of Williamsburg.

Randolph stood out not only for his quick mind, his enviable background, and his notable talent as a public speaker, but also for his distinguished appearance. He was six feet tall and handsome, wearing his dark hair loose, unpowdered, and brushed back from his forehead. In 1786, he was elected governor of Virginia and, in the following year, he was chosen as a delegate to the Constitutional Convention in Philadelphia. There, his state's delegates selected him to present the Virginia Plan for a new government to the convention—the plan that formed the basis for the Constitution that finally was adopted.

Thus it was a surprise when the proposed Constitution came before the delegates for their signatures that Randolph refused to sign. He said he opposed the "indefinite and dangerous power" given to Congress and he favored amendments to be made by state conventions. He suggested another federal convention to consider those amendments before adopting the Constitution because he felt that the necessary nine states would not ratify the document as it stood. His objections failed to sway the prevailing majority.

Then when the Constitution came before the Virginia state convention for ratification, Randolph again caused waves of shock and surprise. He said that because eight states had already ratified the document and because many of them had supported amendments to be added, he now favored ratifying the Constitution. It was a question, he said, of Union or no Union. By a close vote, eighty-nine to seventy-nine, Virginia did ratify the Constitution, but suggested twenty amendments to it as well.

Randolph's flip-flops apparently did not harm him politically. After Washington named him as the nation's first attorney general, he gave up his post as governor of Virginia and embarked on his strange new career mixing public and private legal work. It was in his role as a lawyer for a private individual that Randolph became a key figure in *Chisholm* v. *Georgia*.

In this first major controversial case to reach the Supreme

Court, Randolph argued that Georgia clearly could be sued by a nonresident for the payment of debts. To back up his claim, he cited Article III of the Constitution, which gave the federal courts jurisdiction over controversies between a state and a citizen of another state. John Jay and other members of the Court agreed with him, setting off a confrontation between state and federal power.

Georgia's lawmakers were so furious at what they saw as an improper invasion of the state's sovereignty that they passed a law making any federal officer who attempted to carry out the *Chisholm* decision subject to "death, without benefit of clergy, by hanging." Other states, eager to end the possibility that they, too, would be compelled to pay their debts by a federal court, supported Georgia.

In a short time, the states prevailed upon Congress to pass an amendment to the Constitution reducing the power of the federal courts, explicitly reversing what its framers had written. The Eleventh Amendment, ratified by the states in 1795, says:

> The Judicial power of the United States shall not be construed to extend to any suit in law or equity, commenced or prosecuted against one of the United States by Citizens of another State, or by Citizens or Subjects of any Foreign State.

Nevertheless, the *Chisholm* v. *Georgia* decision by the Supreme Court set an important precedent. Under the leadership of John Jay, its first chief justice, the Court had made its first assertion of its role as the main interpreter of the Constitution. It laid the groundwork for the famous decisions of John Marshall's Supreme Court during the early 1800s defining the Court's power to declare state and federal laws unconstitutional.

9

Hamilton Takes Command

FROM THE DAY HE TOOK OFFICE as the first secretary of the treasury on September 11, 1789, Alexander Hamilton was the most important man in the new United States government after President Washington. His power lay in three factors: The Treasury Department was the biggest arm of the government; he was an intimate adviser to Washington; and he was able, ambitious, and audacious, not afraid to use the powers of his office to affect the course of affairs.

At the age of thirty-four, Hamilton was a man of slender build, five foot seven in height, with an erect military bearing. He was always dressed fashionably, but he was stiff and formal in manner. While his friends thought him generous, eloquent, and charming, there were others who called him vain and arrogant, because he had little patience with fools or those who could not keep up with him intellectually.

Not interested in being popular with the masses of the people, Hamilton liked the company of the rich, the well-born, and the educated. Even though he had been a prime mover in the adoption of the Constitution, he believed in a government fashioned somewhat along the British model, with leadership provided by an elite class. He felt no doubt about his own qualifications for belonging in the select group of rulers.

Yet Hamilton had begun his life most inauspiciously. Born on the Caribbean island of Nevis in 1755, he grew up under the stigma of being the son of an unmarried pair of lovers—a less than prosperous Scottish merchant and the unhappy wife of a German businessman. Early in Hamilton's youth, his father returned to Europe, leaving him with his mother. So the boy began working as a clerk in a counting house at the age of twelve. When he was seventeen, he wrote such an effective description of a hurricane for the *Royal Danish American Gazette* that his friends decided that he should further his education in New York. Soon he was enrolled at Kings College, taking up his pen to defend the rights of the colonists against the British.

When the Revolutionary War broke out, Hamilton became a captain of artillery. Because of his writing ability, he was invited by General George Washington, the commander in chief, to serve as one of his military aides, rising to the rank of lieutenant colonel at the age of twenty-two. Not only was he one of Washington's closest advisers, but he became acquainted with many political leaders, including New York's Philip Schuyler, whose daughter Elizabeth he later married.

Throughout the war, Hamilton was in a key position to observe more than just its military aspects. He was particularly struck by the deterioration of the economy of the united colonies, with a Continental Congress unable to raise money to pay its soldiers. He saw the paper money issued by the Congress sink in value so rapidly that the phrase "not worth a Continental" became popular. Unable to purchase supplies with paper money, the army began to issue certificates of payment, which soon declined in value, too. Hamilton became convinced that the future of an independent nation rested on stopping inflation and restoring the people's confidence in its money.

After the war, Hamilton studied law, then served for a brief time as collector of Continental taxes for the state of New York and as a member of the Continental Congress. His experiences in war and in the early days of peace made him feel more sure that only a strong central government with powers to act for the national interest could establish prosperity. With James Madison, he was a leader in calling the federal convention that adopted the Constitution in 1787. With Madison and John Jay, he wrote *The Federalist*, which provided the main intellectual arguments for ratification of the Constitution. He also served as the leader of the pro-Constitution forces that narrowly prevailed at the New York State ratification convention.

Prepared by all this experience, Hamilton stood ready to take over as the nation's first secretary of the treasury when Washington offered him the post in 1789. The Treasury was the largest of all the government departments. Under his immediate direction, Hamilton had dozens of assistants—including a controller, auditors, and numerous clerks. In addition, he supervised hundreds of customs house officers, internal revenue agents, and post office employees.

Of all the problems the new nation faced, the most chaotic, complex, and important was the state of its finances. Its credit was poor, the nation was deep in debt, and the people had no faith in its money. The nation's debt was staggering for those days—well over $75 million. The debt fell into three categories: Foreign, national, and state.

During the Revolutionary War, the United States had re-

ceived loans from France, totaling about $8 million; and
from private bankers in Holland, about $2 million. With in-
terest, these debts totaled about $12 million. No one dis-
agreed that these foreign loans had to be paid back without
question.

The domestic national debt stood higher, more than $40
million. The Continental Congress had issued paper money,
which was now almost worthless. It also had issued bonds
called "loan office certificates" to raise funds and had authorized officers in the field to supply and pay soldiers with
promissory notes. There was also accrued interest on these
notes and certificates, adding to the total owed.

Finally, there was the debt of the individual states, which
had had the power during the war to raise money and spend
it. After the war, some of the states started to pay off their
debts; others were unable to do so. No one really knew how
much the states owed, but it was a large amount, between
$20 million and $25 million.

A great debate on the national debt started on August 18,
1789, when a group of creditors in Pennsylvania asked Congress to start paying long-overdue interest on the borrowed
money. Since it was near the end of the first session of Congress, the matter was referred to the secretary of the treasury. He was instructed to prepare a report on ways of
supporting the public credit.

Hamilton seized the opportunity. When Congress reconvened in January, he was ready. His "Report on the Public
Credit," despite its bland title, turned out to be one of the
great state papers in American history. It not only set off a
furious controversy but it also started a frenzied round of
financial speculation and a division of contending political
forces that ultimately led to the rise of political parties, as we
shall see in Chapter 10.

The gallery of the House of Representatives was crowded with speculators anxious to find out about government plans when Hamilton's report was formally received on January 14, 1790. Hamilton himself could not be present, in accordance with the rules of the House, so a clerk read the document aloud. It boldly proposed that the federal government pay all the foreign creditors and all those who held notes or paper issued by the previous Continental Congress—as well as assume all the debts owed by the states in 1790.

With Hamilton's controversial report, two specialized words ordinarily used only by students of economics entered the political arena: *Funding*, which meant pledging a certain part of the government's revenue to the payment of interest and principal on the federal debt, and *assumption*, which meant taking over and paying the debts of the states.

Hamilton's objective was a strong, stable government with a high credit rating. To achieve that, in his view, required the support of the propertied class—mostly city merchants—even if it also meant enriching speculators who bought up government notes and obligations at much less than their face value.

As soon as word of Hamilton's plan became public, speculators—including some members of Congress and his own assistant secretary of the treasury, William Duer—did indeed begin to buy up old certificates of obligation. Only a few days later, horse-drawn carriages sped to the South to purchase notes from farmers and others who had not yet heard of the plan. Two ships, chartered by a member of Congress, sailed south carrying agents supplied with money to buy as many notes as they could. The speculators included Robert Morris, who was Hamilton's chief supporter in the Senate, and Fisher Ames, his most eloquent defender in the House of Representatives. But even his most critical

Alexander Hamilton was a controversial but brilliant secretary of the treasury. Portrait by John Trumbull. *The National Portrait Gallery, Smithsonian Institution; gift of Henry Cabot Lodge.*

opponents did not doubt the honesty of Hamilton himself or accuse him of being personally involved in any speculation. His motive was solely that of building a strong financial base for the new nation.

Aside from the fact that the government had a legal responsibility for the debt, Hamilton felt that only by paying it off in full could the government set a firm foundation for economic expansion. As a moral obligation, he said, the "debt of the United States was the price of liberty." Displaying optimism about the future, Hamilton took the position that a tariff on foreign goods entering the country could furnish enough revenue to pay off foreign creditors and meet the current expenses of government.

But how would the rest of the revolutionary debt be paid? By funding—that is, by selling new bonds to raise the required amount of money. For all practical purposes, the holders of almost worthless old securities would simply trade these in and receive, in return, new interest-paying certificates backed by the new government.

Hamilton's proposal resulted in two separate debates in Congress, one on funding, the other on assumption. Although Hamilton was not permitted to speak on the floor of either chamber, he served as the general behind the forces favoring his plan. While he had expected to meet opposition, he was stunned when the leader of the campaign against his plan turned out to be an old associate, James Madison of Virginia, the most powerful man in the House of Representatives.

As Madison arose to speak in the House, visitors in the gallery might have been disappointed by the appearance of such an important leader. In contrast to the dapper Hamilton, Madison was plain in speech and appearance. A small man, with a balding head, he customarily dressed in sober black. Mild in manner, he spoke softly, almost inaudibly. Yet he was formidable in debate because of his grasp of facts and logic, bolstered by exceptional knowledge of political philosophy.

Madison had been one of a key trio of men largely responsible for the adoption of the Constitution. A trusted adviser to Washington, he, along with Hamilton, had led the call for the Constitutional Convention in 1787. He had been the chief architect of the Virginia Plan, which was the foundation of the Constitution, and worked so effectively at the convention that even in his own day he was called "the father of the Constitution." During the ratification struggles, he and Hamilton and John Jay had written *The Federalist* with its compelling arguments in support of the Constitution. In a striking parallel, Madison had been the strong force in convincing Virginia to ratify the Constitution, just as Hamilton had been in New York.

Thus it shocked Hamilton to find that his old colleague opposed his funding plan. Although the two men agreed on the necessity for a strong national government, they disagreed basically in their philosophy of how that government was to work. Madison had no confidence in a government that depended for its support on the greed of its supporters. Hamilton, though, was willing to convert that greed into backing for the new government. Madison was afraid that if Hamilton's plan was adopted, "the moneyed few" would oppress the "industrious and uninformed mass of the people." Madison believed in justice from the government, Hamilton in power.

A further complication for Madison was the political picture in his home state of Virginia. His strong support of the national government was not shared by all the voters of Virginia. There, Anti-Federalists controlled local politics, with

James Madison brilliantly led the House of Representatives in the first Congress. His likeness has been rendered here by Chester Harding. *The National Portrait Gallery, Smithsonian Institution.*

Patrick Henry, still a fiery orator, their leader. They had defeated Madison as a candidate for the Senate, even though he later was elected a representative. Madison well knew that if he endorsed Hamilton's plan he would almost certainly fail to be reelected.

In his speech, Madison matched Hamilton's concern for paying the debt, but he insisted that the real question was: Who should be paid? He criticized the plan to pay the current holders of the debt, the speculators, and charged that they had defrauded widows, orphans, and soldiers, who had sold notes without knowing of the plan to repay them. Was it fair for the federal government to gain the support of the rich by losing the affection of the people? Would it not be better to adopt a compromise whereby purchasers of the securities, mostly speculators, would be repaid at their market value while the original holders would receive the remainder?

The answer by Congress was no. It voted down Madison's compromise by a vote of thirty-six to thirteen, mainly because of fear that it would be too complicated to find the original holders and more costly than Hamilton's plan. But the debate had important results for the future. Madison won a reputation throughout the country as a champion of the common man fighting against the moneyed interests, always a popular image. As Hamilton himself later said, the debate laid the foundation for the "great schism" that resulted in the development of American political parties.

But Madison had only lost the first round, the battle over funding the debt. There remained the second part of Hamilton's plan, the assumption of the state debts by Congress. That battle was longer and more complicated because the interests of the various states diverged so much. It set up a confrontation between the northern states and the southern states for two simple reasons: Most of the speculators were in the commercial North, and the states with the largest amount of unpaid debts were in the North. Massachusetts had the greatest debt of all, whereas Virginia and other southern states had raised money by taxation as well as borrowing and, therefore, owed less.

Assumption was a key element in Hamilton's plan. Not only would it contribute to a more orderly and stable arrangement of national finances, he contended, but it would also consolidate the interests of all the states to create a national political unity. His opponents, however, claimed that assumption would diminish the importance of the states and, as Patrick Henry said, would establish "the subserviency of Southern to Northern interests."

With opposition to assumption strong, Hamilton rallied his forces. Two members of Congress, one lame, the other sick, were carried to the floor of the House of Representatives to vote on the issue. Another, planning to leave town, was asked to stay to cast his ballot. Speculators were active, and government officials left their desks to lobby for the measure as letters poured in opposing it. For weeks, Hamilton, fearful that he might lose, kept instructing his supporters to postpone action by Congress.

When the measure at last was voted on, Hamilton lost by a narrow margin. Yet that decision was not final. On five different occasions, the assumption bill was rejected by the House of Representatives, but each time the vote was so close that Hamilton felt encouraged to believe that he could still win. He rejected a proposal to defer the vote until the next session of Congress because he thought a postponement would throw the credit market into a panic and his whole plan would lose. But how could he swing the necessary votes to his side?

At that crucial time for Hamilton, another major player entered the political scene. In late March, a local newspaper reported: "On Sunday last, arrived in this city, Thomas Jefferson, Esq., Secretary of State for the United States of America." Jefferson, who had been abroad for five years as the American minister in Paris, had now returned home to take up his position in Washington's cabinet alongside Hamilton. The two men were strangers, knowing each other only by reputation.

They met one morning as they both were arriving for a meeting with Washington, and they stayed outside talking together. Jefferson reported the conversation this way:

> He walked me backwards and forwards before the President's door for half an hour. He painted pathetically the temper into which the legislature had been wrought; the disgust of those who were called the creditor states; the danger of the secession of their members; and the separation of the states. He observed that the members of the administration ought to act in concert; that though the question was not of my department, yet a common duty should make it a common concern . . . it was probable that an appeal from me to the judgement and discretion of some of my friends might effect a change in the vote, and the machine of government, now suspended, might again be set in motion.

Jefferson replied that he was a stranger to the subject but concerned about anything that might involve a dissolution of the Union. He invited Hamilton to dinner the next evening, together with some of his own friends. At the dinner, Hamilton threw into the conversation his last bargaining chip, the site of a new capital for the United States. Everyone knew that New York was only the temporary capital and that a more centrally located one would sooner or later be chosen. Hamilton had already tried to bargain votes for assumption by moving the capital to Pennsylvania, but the Pennsylvania delegates could not agree among themselves about where it should be.

At the dinner, attended by Madison as well as Jefferson and Hamilton, a political bargain was struck. What would it take to obtain the necessary southern votes? Madison and Jefferson, fellow Virginians and close political associates, set the price: A permanent location for the new national capital on the banks of the Potomac River. Hamilton accepted. Since the votes of the Pennsylvania delegation were important, too, it was further agreed that Philadelphia would be the temporary capital for ten years until the permanent site of the government was completed.

Accordingly, on August 5, 1790, the assumption bill passed. Two Virginia representatives, Richard Bland Lee and Alexander White, whose districts bordered on the Potomac River—where the new capital would be—had been convinced they should change their votes to favor assumption. Madison accepted the bargain because he felt that "the crisis demands the spirit of accommodation." Jefferson said he could see "the necessity of yielding to the cries of the creditors . . . for the sake of the Union, and to save it from the greatest of all calamities, the total extinction of our credit in Europe." For Hamilton, who did not care much where the capital was located, it was the triumph of his financial plans for the nation.

With Hamilton's funding and assumption measures now law, the securities that once were "not worth a Continental" increased in real value. One estimate is that the speculators made a profit of about $40 million, thus cementing them and the commercial interests of the North behind Hamilton and his policies. But the agrarian interests, mainly in the South, felt that they had become the victims of speculators, bankers, and northern politicians.

Even though the federal government was now saddled with a debt of more than $75 million, Hamilton insisted that the country had never been in better financial shape. He viewed the debt as an instrument for growth—claiming that it tied affluent citizens, and even foreign investors, to the success of the new government. Because they would earn interest on the money they loaned to the government, investors would have strong personal reasons for supporting it. Furthermore, by buying new bonds backed by the government, investors would provide the funds to pay the government's expenses and foster a healthy climate for private economic growth.

When the second session of the first Congress adjourned in August, 1790, Hamilton, at the peak of his power and popularity, was well satisfied with what he had accomplished—and ready to proceed with a more ambitious financial program for the nation. But Jefferson felt less satisfied. To him, the debt controversy had been an introduction to the new world of politics at home, a world in which he was soon to find himself not only the secretary of state but also the leader of the opposition to Hamilton's policies.

10

The Rise of Political Parties

IN JULY OF 1789, THOMAS JEFFERSON had been in Paris as the United States minister to France, watching the daily events of the French Revolution. Riding in his carriage on July 12, he saw the people using stones to attack the mounted soldiers of the king. The next day, the French Assembly asked King Louis XVI for arms to preserve order in the city, but he refused to heed its request. On the tumultuous day of July 14, the French people stormed the prison they called the Bastille, took all the arms, freed the prisoners, and executed the officers in charge.

When Jefferson sailed home a few months later, he returned to a nation that had already gone through its revolution and was now constructing a new government peacefully. At the age of forty-seven, Jefferson took the oath of office as the first secretary of state of the United States on March 22, 1790. Along with his official foreign affairs duties, he soon emerged as the leader of a growing opposition to the domestic policies of Treasury Secretary Alexander Hamilton, who had already become President Washington's principal adviser.

At that time, there were no organized national political parties in the United States. In fact, almost everyone in government opposed the idea of political parties. Washington himself had said, "If we mean to support liberty and independence, which it has cost us so much blood and treasure to establish, we must drive away the demon of party spirit . . ." Vice President Adams expressed the prevailing opinion: "There is nothing I dread so much as the division of the Republic into two great parties, each under its leader . . . This, in my humble opinion, is to be feared as the greatest political evil under our Constitution."

But the founders of the nation were realists. They recognized that conflicts existed between competing interests. Just before the Constitutional Convention in 1787, James Madison had written:

> All civilized societies are divided into different interests and factions as they happen to be creditors or debtors, rich or poor—husbandmen, merchants or manufacturers—members of different religious sects—followers of different leaders— owners of different kinds of property, etc. etc. In republican government, the majority, however composed, ultimately give the law. Whenever, therefore, an apparent interest or common passion unites a majority, what is to restrain them from unjust violations of the rights and interests of the minority or of individuals?

What Madison expected was that the competing factions composed of various interest groups would combine in merely temporary alliances as various issues developed. He thought that these alliances would dissolve when a new issue arose, and different alliances would develop. Neither he nor

Thomas Jefferson was serving as minister to France when George
Washington appointed him Secretary of State. Portrait by Charles
Willson Peale. *Independence National Historical Park Collection*.

any of the other Founding Fathers imagined that interest groups would unite in permanent alliances—in effect, form political parties—competing for power in government.

During the fight to ratify the Constitution, the roots of two major political forces became clear. As the state conventions began to debate the new Constitution, those favoring it called themselves Federalists; and those opposed, Anti-Federalists. In reality, the Federalists were nationalists who favored a strong central government while the Anti-Federalists supported strong state governments and a weak national government.

The Federalists were a loose association of interests— merchants, shippers, lawyers, and speculators in both land and securities who saw economic benefit to themselves and the nation generally in the new national government. By and large, they were creditors, more likely to have money owed to them than to owe money themselves. Their strength lay in the commercial centers along the Atlantic seaboard, especially in the North.

At the core of the Anti-Federalists were the independent farmers of the interior, who at that time constituted the vast majority of the population, perhaps as much as 90 percent. But the Anti-Federalists included debtors of all kinds as well as those deeply concerned about the threat posed to individual liberties by a powerful central government. Their arguments against the new Constitution centered on its lack of a bill of rights, although they also objected to some of the powers of the new president and the new Congress.

It was a victory for the Federalists when the Constitution was ratified, but only a narrow victory. They won only because they made a major concession to the Anti-Federalists, promising to add a bill of rights as amendments to the Constitution. As we have seen in Chapter 7, that promise was kept. Thus, the dispute between the two powerful political groups had produced a positive result—the Bill of Rights that protects our civil liberties today.

Despite the great division of political opinion during the years when the new government came into being, no formal political parties existed, except in a few states. President George Washington considered himself above factions, and so did most of the people. Nevertheless, Washington's chief aide, Alexander Hamilton, had the instincts of a shrewd politician—and it was he who built the nation's first national political party, the Federalists.

Even before Hamilton took office as the nation's first secretary of the treasury, he had arrived at this conclusion: "As a general marches at the head of his troops, so ought wise politicians, if I dare use the phrase, to march at the head of affairs . . . They ought not to wait the event, to know what measures to take; but the measures which they have taken, ought to produce the event."

So he seized the opportunity in his "Report on the Public Credit" to advocate paying all federal and state debts at face value. This produced a schism between Hamilton and his old associate, Madison, who became the first leading spokesman for the agrarian interests opposing the Hamiltonian program.

Throughout the months of debate on successive Hamiltonian proposals—funding the Continental debt, assumption of state debts, and the creation of a Bank of the United States—the opposition of the farming community increased. The great tobacco planters of Virginia, who were perpetually in debt, joined with struggling farmers farther inland to oppose the threatening money power of the new federal establishment. Thus, at the very beginning of the nation, an unlikely collaboration began between southern gentry and small, self-sufficient farmers. This partnership would later form the nucleus of the Democratic party of Andrew Jackson and Franklin D. Roosevelt, but its earliest manifestation was the Democratic-Republican party of Madison and Jefferson. In those days, its name was often shortened to Republican, although it had no connection with the Republican party of today.

The philosopher of the early agrarian opposition was a Virginia planter, John Taylor, who owned thousands of acres and scores of slaves. He believed that Hamilton's policies were creating a new class of "parasites"—the moneyed aristocracy in the cities—which was siphoning wealth from the American farmer. Taylor and his supporters went one step further, calling all Federalists "parasites"; for them, those who labored on the earth were "the chosen people of God," in Jefferson's phrase.

To start with, the leadership of the Anti-Federalist forces fell to Madison because of his active role in the House of Representatives. Before his supporters became known as the Democratic-Republicans, they were sometimes called "the Madisonians." Jefferson's great contribution to this cause came a little later and then mostly behind the scenes, owing to his preference for working through others. He wrote letters rather than making speeches, so much so that one historian, John C. Miller, said, "In part, at least, Jefferson was a political leader through the grace of the United States mails."

The clash between the Federalist and Democratic-Republican philosophies of government was most clearly revealed in the disagreement between Hamilton and Jefferson about whether President Washington should sign or veto a bill to establish a Bank of the United States. In December of 1790, Hamilton proposed such a bank, which would serve as a depository for United States funds, act as the fiscal agent of the

The First Bank of the United States was erected in Philadelphia following Alexander Hamilton's proposals in 1791. Print by William Birch in *The City of Philadelphia, in the State of Pennsylvania, as it appeared in the Year 1800. The Historical Society of Pennsylvania*.

Treasury Department, and issue paper money to take the place of gold and silver coins. Among the Federalists, such a bank seemed essential to promote the continued economic growth of the nation. The Democratic-Republicans felt certain, though, that the bank would provide another mechanism for the rich to get richer by helping businessmen rather than farmers.

Despite Madison's doubts about whether the Constitution permitted the creation of such a bank, the bank bill passed by a close margin. But Madison succeeded in raising a question in Washington's mind and so the president, as was his custom, consulted his cabinet secretaries for their opinions on the matter before deciding whether or not to sign the measure.

Jefferson held that the bill was clearly unconstitutional because creating a bank was not one of the powers delegated to the federal government by the Constitution. He contended that the central government was sharply limited by the language of the Constitution, with the states retaining their sovereign power, except where the Constitution specifically delegated certain powers to Congress or the president. Jefferson's arguments impressed Washington, who told Hamilton that he could not approve the bill unless Hamilton could effectively rebut Jefferson's arguments.

Hamilton realized that a major constitutional question had arisen—a question larger than merely the fate of the bank. He, therefore, took great pains in preparing his reply. He insisted that no Constitution could possibly enumerate all the powers needed to meet emergencies and that it would be folly to restrain the government by a strict interpretation of the Constitution. "Unexpected invasions, long and ruinous wars may demand all the possible abilities of the country," he wrote. "The contingencies of society are not reducible to calculations. They cannot be fixed or bounded, even in imagination."

Then Hamilton went further with a broad interpretation of one phrase in the Constitution. In Article I, following a list of specific powers granted to the Congress, the document says: "[The Congress shall have Power] . . . to make all Laws which shall be necessary and proper for carrying into Execution the foregoing Powers . . ." According to Hamilton, the words "necessary and proper" really meant "needful, useful or conducive to." Since a bank was necessary for regulating trade, he argued, creating a bank fell within the constitutional powers of Congress. In short, Hamilton felt that the federal government had the right to employ all means "necessary and proper" to attain any objective not specifically forbidden by the Constitution or not contrary to the essential ends of society.

Although Hamilton did not satisfy all of Washington's objections, his assertion of the validity of the implied powers for the government convinced the president to sign the bill creating the bank. Two hundred years later, it is clear that both sides in that early debate had good grounds for their arguments. When the bank began operating, it did favor the merchants and businessmen who were the core of the Federalist party, while failing to help the nation's farmers. Nevertheless, the bank actually became an important instrument fostering the growth of the United States. More important in the long run, Hamilton's argument defending the constitutionality of the implied powers of the federal government would be used later by many other presidents, including Jefferson himself, and is accepted today without question.

But the discord between Jefferson and Hamilton was not restricted to arguments about fine points of the Constitution. In essence, they were struggling for political power, particularly to influence the decisions of President Washington on foreign as well as domestic matters. Hamilton himself defined the differences between the two men and their supporters:

> One side appears to believe that there is a serious plot to overturn the State governments, and substitute a monarchy to the present Republican system. The other side firmly believes that there is a serious plot to overturn the general government and elevate the separate powers of the States upon its ruins. Both sides may be equally wrong.

In fact, both sides were wrong. There were no plots to overturn any government, federal or state. But real differences existed between the policies of the two parties, their leaders, and their supporters. The Federalists were united by a common interest in property and a common distrust of the mass of the people. The Democratic-Republicans were a loose association of varied state political forces, drawn together by their opposition to bankers and their belief that agriculture must be the basis for prosperity in a democratic society.

To keep in touch with their supporters, each of the parties operated a newspaper. In those days before radio or television, or even the telephone, newspapers served as the basic means of informing the public. Most papers then were weeklies sent by mail to distant parts of the United States.

Among the twelve newspapers published in Philadelphia in 1791, the most important was the *Gazette of the United States*, with the largest national circulation of its era. Its editor was John Fenno, a native of Boston, who had been a schoolteacher and a journalist there before he founded the *Gazette* in Philadelphia. It seems indisputable that Federalist leaders provided the financial backing that enabled him to publish his newspaper.

They got their money's worth. In every issue, the *Gazette* praised Federalist policies and extolled the talents of Alexander Hamilton. It received printing jobs from the Treasury Department, and Hamilton even lent money to the editor. For Jefferson, the *Gazette of the United States* was "a paper of pure Toryism, disseminating the doctrines of monarchy, aristocracy and the exclusion of the influence of the people."

To counteract the *Gazette of the United States*, Jefferson and Madison resolved to publish their own newspaper. In 1791, they persuaded Philip Freneau, already noted as the

"poet of the Revolution," to start another paper in Philadelphia, the *National Gazette*. Freneau had more fame than
money, though. To help pay his expenses, he was appointed
a clerk in Jefferson's State Department at a salary of $250 a
year.

Freneau had a gift for biting satire. Born in New York
City, he had been a schoolmate of Madison's at Princeton,
where he wrote savage anti-British poetry. During the Revolution, he was made a prisoner of war by the British, an
experience that solidified his hatred for England. After the
war, he used his pen to attack monarchy, the aristocrats, and
the Federalists. He delighted in blasting Hamilton personally while describing Jefferson as "that illustrious patriot,
statesman and philosopher."

Those two Founding Fathers were opposites in personality
as well as in politics. Hamilton was small, elegant, and ag-
gressive while Jefferson was tall, untidy, and somewhat diffi-
dent. Hamilton admired the British government and the
British; Jefferson disliked the British and admired the
French. Their major difference, though, was in how they
viewed the people. Hamilton has been quoted as saying,
"Your people, sir, is a great beast." By contrast, Jefferson
believed that "The voice of the people is the voice of God."
Ironically, it was Jefferson, an aristocrat by birth and manner, who championed more democracy while Hamilton,
born poor and obliged to work as a boy, spoke for the elite,
the financial interests.

Yet both men shared one undignified trait. In private talks
with President Washington, each high official warned him
against the other. They even argued in front of Washington
at cabinet meetings. Jefferson told Washington that
Hamilton was responsible for the growth of a get-rich-quick
mania dangerous to the nation as a whole. Hamilton fur-

nished Washington with a bill of complaints against Jefferson, picturing him as an enemy of the administration's policies, with a "lust for power." Jefferson himself referred to the conflict with a touch of humor when he remarked, "Hamilton and myself were daily pitted in the Cabinet like two cocks."

For Washington, it was a painful turn of events to have his two principal advisers arguing both publicly and privately. He once wrote to Jefferson: "I believe the views of both of you to be pure and well-meant. I have a great, a sincere esteem and regard for both of you and ardently wish that some line could be marked out by which both [of] you could walk." Washington urged the two men to make "mutual yieldings," but they were adamant. Hamilton, in effect, dared the president: Choose between us. Jefferson, on the other hand, offered to resign if it was made clear that his retirement had not been forced by Hamilton.

But Washington needed them both. He inclined toward Hamilton's views, but he was not a dedicated Federalist. He also admired Jefferson and, as one historian has pointed out, by keeping Jefferson in the cabinet the president deprived him of complete freedom to organize opposition to the government. Moreover, both Hamilton and Jefferson drew back from an outright break, because of their great admiration for President Washington. In the end, Washington's pleas for at least surface harmony prevailed, even though the newspaper war of words continued.

During the spring of 1792, Washington—who saw the presidency as a chore—began to think of retiring once more to Mount Vernon. His health was poor and his memory declining, he said. He asked James Madison to prepare a farewell address for him, but Madison spoke up against it. Such a step would "surprise and shock the public," he said.

For once Jefferson and Hamilton agreed. They saw Washington as the glue that held the nation together and begged him to accept another term. Reluctantly, he consented.

Washington was elected unanimously in 1792 as he had been in 1789. But the spirit of harmony did not universally prevail. John Adams, again the Federalist candidate for vice president, got seventy-seven votes, while George Clinton, the governor of New York who was the Democratic-Republican candidate, came close with fifty votes. In various states, too, the Democratic-Republicans showed new strength by electing additional members of the House of Representatives, although the Federalists still retained control.

So the nation's political complexion obviously was changing, even if the change was scarcely noticeable. Only with the hindsight of history would it become clear that the Democratic-Republican party had already begun growing in importance while the Federalists were starting to decline.

11

Moving Day

BACK IN AUGUST OF 1790, President Washington had left New York for the last time. Escorted by federal and state officials, he and his wife ceremoniously boarded an elaborate barge to cross the Hudson River. Thirteen oarsmen in white jackets and black caps, one representing each state of the Union, pulled at their oars as their journey began. First, the Washingtons were going home for a visit to Mount Vernon— and then they would resume their official life in Philadelphia, the new capital of the United States.

Before he departed from New York, Washington had assigned the process of moving his furniture to Tobias Lear, his secretary. In Philadelphia, the city had appropriated the house of Washington's old friend, Robert Morris, for use as the president's official residence. Washington knew the house well; he had stayed there as a guest during the Constitutional Convention in 1787.

It was a house with an interesting history. Built before the Revolutionary War, it had been General Howe's headquarters while the British occupied the city. Later, Benedict Arnold lived in it. Partly destroyed by fire in 1780, the house had been rebuilt by Morris into what local residents called the finest single residence in the city. Morris was a rich man, and his three-story brick home, with its lavish furnishings, reflected his wealth. Besides its spacious rooms, it also had a hothouse for growing exotic fruits, an icehouse, and stables in back with stalls for a dozen horses.

Washington inspected the property on his way southward to Mount Vernon—and, surprisingly, found it wanting. It was, he acknowledged, the best residence in the city, but nevertheless "inadequate to the commodious accommodation of my family." He described the house in a letter to Tobias Lear:

> The first floor contains only two public rooms . . . The second floor will have two public rooms, and with the aid of one room with the partition in it in the back building, will be sufficient for the accommodation of Mrs. Washington and the children, and their maids, besides affording me a small place for a private study and dressing room. The third story will furnish you and Mrs. Lear with a good lodging room, a public office (for there is no place below for one), and two rooms for gentlemen of the family.

But Washington, worried about the proper care of his horses, insisted on as high standards for their housing as for his own home. "There are good stables," he wrote to Lear, "but for twelve horses only. . . ." It turned out, however, that the stable facilities could actually accommodate sixteen horses without crowding and so, after all, would meet the President's needs.

By early November, the house had been renovated with new bow windows on the southern exposure and had been

At the end of George Washington's second and final term as president, Edward Savage painted *The Washington Family. National Gallery of Art, Washington; Andrew W. Mellon Collection.*

freshly painted to welcome the Washingtons. The president arrived there on November 27, 1790, and immediately began to receive important guests. Already, many members of Congress had arrived in the city in preparation for the new session that would meet on December 6.

In 1790, Philadelphia was the largest city in the United States, with a population of 42,500. It stretched for about nine blocks north and south between the Delaware and Schuylkill rivers, with tidy red-brick houses facing red-brick foot pavements. Even the roadways had been paved with pebbles. Planted along both sides of each street were handsome buttonwood, willow, and Lombardy poplar trees.

During years past, Philadelphia had often been host to

government gatherings, so the city now seemed familiar to many members of Congress and to Washington himself. It was there in 1775 that the Continental Congress had named him to be commander in chief of the Continental Army, and it was there in 1787 that he presided over the Constitutional Convention. Philadelphia was the nation's leading center for commerce and the arts, and with the arrival of Congress it also became the nation's social as well as political capital.

The city's residents welcomed the federal government warmly, even though they knew that Philadelphia would be the capital of the nation for ten years only—until the government's permanent home could be built on the banks of the Potomac River farther south. Meanwhile, Philadelphia had erected a new city hall for itself on the corner of Chestnut and Sixth Streets, to the west of Independence Hall. The building, completed in 1789, had been fixed up for Congress and became known as Congress Hall. It was (and still is) a graceful two-story red-brick building in the Georgian style, with a cupola and a weather vane on top.

Inside this handsome structure, late in 1790, the House of Representatives met in a chamber that occupied almost the entire first floor. The members sat at desks in three semicircular rows facing the Speaker's chair. The Senate met in a smaller chamber on the second floor, which also contained rooms for committee meetings. In a very plain chair in front of a mahogany table draped with green silk, Vice President Adams presided over the Senate, whose members sat on mahogany chairs arranged in semicircles.

Behind Congress Hall lay a garden designed by Samuel Vaughan, a former merchant of London and a friend of Washington's. Two doors at the rear of the House chamber often were left open to permit members to retreat to the garden for informal talks while debate continued on the floor. Not far away was the strange museum established by the well-known portrait painter Charles Willson Peale. It was one of the city's most notable points of interest, filled with practically everything imaginable, from magic mirrors to stuffed birds, as well as portraits of just about every prominent American citizen.

Peale, born in Maryland in 1741, had been apprenticed to a saddle maker at the age of thirteen. He liked painting better, though, and by his twenties was traveling around the colonies supporting himself by fixing saddles while trying to convince people that they ought to pay him for painting their portraits. While serving as a soldier at Valley Forge during the Revolutionary War, he had recorded much of what he saw on canvas.

Peale's aim, he wrote to one of his many friends, was to preserve for posterity the "remembrance of the worthies of my time." Thus, he seized every opportunity to paint portraits of the leading figures in the new government. Yet the sums he earned from his art proved insufficient to feed a family that eventually included eleven children. As a result, he turned his inventive mind to finding an alternate source of income.

Around the time of the Constitutional Convention, he had caused quite a stir by setting up an exhibit of "moving pictures"—transparent paintings that could be manipulated and lighted in a manner to produce the illusion of a realistic scene. When ticket sales slowed, he conceived the grander idea of establishing a museum of natural history as well as art. Opened in July of 1788, this turned into a remarkably lasting attraction—with a five-legged cow, a rattlesnake with fifteen rattles, Indian scalps, and mastodon jawbones. When

Peale died in 1827, most of the items he had assembled were bought by P. T. Barnum for the circus man's own collection of curiosities.

During Philadelphia's brief glory as the nation's capital, Mr. Peale's museum acquired wide renown. But the biggest attraction then was the social life that centered around the president. Despite the pressure of grave problems that faced the new nation, social Philadelphia in the early years of the new republic displayed an air of ostentatious gaiety somewhat at odds with the idea of Quaker simplicity upon which the city had been founded. Abigail Adams, who was a perceptive observer, described the city as "one continued scene of Parties upon Parties, balls and entertainment equal to any European city."

For wealthy Philadelphians, the arrival of the federal government and its leaders provided a splendid opportunity to achieve added social prominence. Foremost among the hosts was William Bingham, a rich Federalist merchant and land speculator who later became a United States senator. But his lively and elegantly dressed wife, Anne Willing Bingham, probably did more to make their home the center of the Philadelphia social elite.

From the couple's European travels, Mrs. Bingham had formed the idea of establishing a salon of her own in Philadelphia, where she could preside over the witty conversation of beautiful women and important political leaders. Her model was the intellectual salons of Paris where, she wrote, "the women of France interfere in the politics of the Country, and often give a decided turn to the Fate of Empires."

And so the Bingham mansion on Spruce Street in Philadelphia became the site of many dinners, balls, and receptions for government officials, aristocrats fleeing the French Revolution, and visiting English notables. Mrs. Bingham's guests walked up a broad marble stairway to a drawing room where chairs with lyre backs were covered in yellow and crimson silk after the latest London fashion, and the walls were papered in the French manner "after the style of the Vatican in Rome."

For some, including Jefferson and Madison, the ostentation of the glittering Bingham salon was too much, reminding them of the social life of a royal court. But Washington's frigid dignity warmed to Mrs. Bingham's sprightly conversation, so the Binghams were the most important social leaders of his administration.

Others entertained, too, among them Robert Morris and Benjamin Chew, members of prominent Philadelphia families. In addition, Senator Pierce Butler of South Carolina maintained a lavish establishment at which southern members of Congress were always welcome. And Senator Aaron Burr of New York gave elegant entertainments, mostly for other politicians. One New Jersey senator wrote to his wife, "There is more gayety here than I wish to partake of."

Washington's own receptions were quite different from the splashy Bingham parties. Following his custom, he received gentlemen at a levee every Tuesday afternoon between three and four o'clock—with the same formality he had already established in New York. A servant conducted visitors to the dining room, from which the table had been removed, where the president stood before the fireplace, usually dressed in a rich black velvet coat and breeches, worn with a white satin vest. Washington bowed to each new arrival, but there were no handshakes or any real conversation throughout the stilted hour.

A similar stiff formality prevailed at the dinners the Washingtons gave every Thursday at four o'clock for friends and members of Congress. But Washington relaxed somewhat when he attended the Friday evening drawing room receptions held by Mrs. Washington for her friends and ladies of the city. She seemed comfortable there, and the president unbent and mingled with the guests.

What he really liked was going out in his big cream-colored coach pulled by a team of long-tailed Virginia bay horses for a drive into the countryside. Even more frequently, Washington relished a noontime walk around town. He seemed quite at ease as he strolled out to set his watch by the Clark's clock at Front and High streets, returning the salute of workmen who took their hats off in respect as he passed.

In the evenings, Washington particularly enjoyed going to the theater. He frequently attended the Southwark Theatre, bringing a large party that filled several boxes for the evening performances that started at six-fifteen. His favorite plays were *The School for Scandal* and a lesser-known comedy, *Poor Soldier*. His attendance was always a signal for a large turnout of local society.

But obviously life in Philadelphia was not merely an endless round of social events. The House of Representatives and the Senate kept busy with affairs of state while the city bustled with commerce. Like all other cities of the late eighteenth century, Philadelphia faced many problems associated with a diverse population, rapid growth, and economic dislocation.

Today, when many cities have over a million in population, it may be difficult to believe that one with only 42,500 residents might have suffered from urban problems. But it did. One newspaper editor of the day complained that Philadelphia was filled with a "swinish multitude." More fair-minded observers recognized that the city, like others along the Atlantic seaboard, confronted a trying challenge as a result of the large number of immigrants from Europe pouring into the United States. During the ten years preceding Philadelphia's becoming the nation's capital, 27,000 immigrants had arrived there, and 13,000 of them, mostly from Ireland, remained in the city, substantially crowding it.

Philadelphia was also a haven for refugees from the black revolution on the Caribbean island of Santo Domingo in 1793. They arrived during hot summer weather—and shortly thereafter an epidemic of the deadly yellow fever erupted. In that period, it was not known that mosquitoes transmitted the disease from person to person, and so for a time it was suspected that a cargo of putrified coffee, dumped by a ship, might have been the cause of the outbreak. People even thought that the disease had been spread by the circulation of pungent air from the coffee spill.

In any case, panic and terror struck the city during the hot days of August. At first business went on as usual, but soon people in every neighborhood showed alarming symptoms— glazed eyes, a yellow complexion, and seizures of vomiting and delirium. Many died within twelve hours after exhibiting the first signs of the disease. By the middle of September, six hundred people had fallen victim to the epidemic.

By then, Philadelphia was a ghost city. Almost all government had been suspended. Business withered because merchants and clerks stayed home. Other seaports refused to accept cargoes from Philadelphia. Thomas Jefferson, who lived outside the city, wrote to his friend James Madison, "Everybody who can, is flying from the city, and the panic of the country people is likely to add famine to the disease" because they would not bring fresh food into the city.

Washington left Philadelphia early in September. Even though he normally went to Mount Vernon at that time of year, his absence increased the demoralization of the remaining residents. "It was my wish to have continued there longer," he wrote to his secretary, Tobias Lear, "but as Mrs. Washington was unwilling to leave me surrounded by the malignant fever which prevailed, I could not think of hazarding her and the children any longer by my continuance in the city, the house in which we lived being, in a manner, blockaded by the disorder, and was becoming every day more and more fatal."

Fear of the disease was so great that, when Alexander Hamilton departed after contracting a mild case, he was shunned almost as a leper as he made his way to Albany. Secretary of War Henry Knox was made to stay in quarantine in New Jersey before he could pass through to his home in Boston.

The doctors of the day knew very little about the treatment of yellow fever. Some like Dr. Benjamin Rush, the best-known physician in town, believed in bloodletting and purging the intestines through drugs. But there were others like Dr. Jean Deveze, more experienced in tropical diseases, who prescribed cleanliness, cool liquids, cool baths, and mild medicines.

Still, the epidemic continued without letup through October—and so did the deaths. The onset of cooler weather did not halt the spread of the disease, as many had expected. One estimate was that one-tenth of the population of Philadelphia—more than five thousand people—died of yellow fever before frost finally ended the epidemic.

President Washington himself had to decide whether the government should return to Philadelphia that autumn. One of the few officials of the federal government who remained in the area, Oliver Wolcott, then controller of the treasury, had moved his home and office to Smith's Folly, a mansion

The historic Deshler-Morris House in Germantown (now a district of Philadelphia) was occupied by George Washington in 1793 when a yellow fever epidemic swept through Philadelphia. *Independence National Park Collection.*

outside the city above the falls of the Schuylkill River. He wrote to Washington in late October that it was still not safe to return to Philadelphia. Washington wrote to James Madison inquiring about the constitutionality of convening Congress in another city.

But on October 18, before he received a reply from Madison, Washington left his wife at home in Mount Vernon and set out for Germantown, outside Philadelphia, where Attorney General Edmund Randolph had found him quarters about six miles from Independence Hall. Happily, a light frost chilled Philadelphia the very evening of Washington's departure from Mount Vernon, and the fever began to abate. With that news, many who had fled the city started returning to pick up their normal lives. At last, the epidemic was over.

Against the advice of his aides, Washington rode into the city on November 10, bowing to the few people he saw on the streets. He noted the fresh, cool air in the city and decided that Congress could safely meet in Philadelphia after all. He went back to Germantown and sent word that he would return to Philadelphia for the opening of Congress in December.

Thereafter, Philadelphia remained the capital of the United States until 1800, when the government moved to the new city of Washington, D.C., on the banks of the Potomac River.

12

Soldiers and Indians

IT WAS A HISTORIC MOMENT—11:30 on the morning of August 22, 1789. For the first time, George Washington entered the chamber of the United States Senate as president to seek its advice and consent about a treaty, in accordance with the Constitution. At issue were instructions to negotiators for a new treaty with the Indian tribes in the South that lived within the borders of the United States but did not recognize the government.

Washington was escorted to the chair of John Adams, the vice president, who presided over the Senate. With the senators seated before him, Washington turned to General Henry Knox, the secretary of war, who accompanied him, and handed him a paper. General Knox, in turn, passed the paper to Adams, who started to read aloud the negotiating points for which Washington was seeking approval.

But a problem arose. Through the windows of the chamber, opened for a breath of air in the summer's heat, the noise of passing carriages rumbled in distractingly. Senator

Robert Morris of Pennsylvania stood up and said the noise was so great that he could not hear the question that had just been read. Could it be repeated? It was the first sign that things were not going well in that notable encounter between the president and the Senate.

The vice president read the question again. "Do you advise and consent?" he asked.

There was a silence. It was broken by Senator William Maclay of Pennsylvania, a suspicious man.

"Mr. President," he said, addressing Adams, the presiding officer, "the paper which you now have read to us appears to have for its basis sundry treaties and public transactions between the Southern Indians and the states of Georgia, North Carolina and South Carolina. The business is new to the Senate. It is of importance. It is our duty to inform ourselves as well as possible on the subject. I therefore call for the reading of the treaties and other documents alluded to in the paper before us."

As he spoke, Maclay looked at Washington. "I saw that he wore an aspect of stern displeasure," Maclay recorded in his diary that night. But Washington remained silent. Maclay whispered to Morris, his fellow senator from Pennsylvania, that he thought the best way to proceed was to have all the relevant papers sent to a committee of the Senate for consideration. Morris agreed and moved that the matter be referred to a Senate committee.

Unexpectedly, President Washington spoke up. "This defeats every purpose of my coming here," he said angrily.

Washington went on to say that he had brought the secretary of war, who handled Indian affairs, to answer questions so that the Senate could proceed without delay. He did not understand why a committee was necessary. As he spoke, he appeared to become calmer and concluded by noting that he had no objection to a short delay. He withdrew from the chamber with "sullen dignity," as Maclay put it.

That encounter was the first confrontation between a president exercising his prerogative to negotiate treaties and a Senate insisting on its right to advise as well as merely consent. Because the Constitution itself sets forth this division of authority, continued friction between the two branches of the federal government charged with treaty-making responsibilities has continued to this day. For Maclay and other senators in the very first Congress, it seemed important to set a precedent favorable to their body. In his diary, Maclay described the confrontation this way:

> The President wishes to tread on the necks of the Senate . . .
> He wishes us to see with the eyes and hear with the ears of
> his Secretary only. The Secretary to advance the premises,
> the President to draw the conclusions, and to bear down our
> deliberations with his personal authority and presence. Form
> only will be left to us. This will not do with Americans.

When Washington returned to the Senate following the delay it had requested, the atmosphere had changed. The president seemed serene, according to Maclay, and the Senate worked out with him the details of the negotiating instructions to be given to the commissioners to the Indians.

It was the first and last time that a president appeared before the Senate in person to ask its advice and consent before negotiating a treaty. As a result, the word *advise* in the constitutional phrase *advise and consent* has become almost meaningless. Although since then some presidents have asked some senators individually for advice, none has asked the Senate as a body to give its advice about a treaty before embarking on negotiations. Over the years, however, problems have often arisen regarding ratification of treaties, for which a two-thirds vote in the Senate is required. Many historians trace the difficulty to Senate resentment over the fact that its advice has not been asked in advance.

Back in 1789, though, the most important fact was that the president and the Senate, despite their difficulties, were actually cooperating on an Indian policy. At that time, the new United States faced west toward a ring of hostile Indian tribes from the Saint Lawrence River south to the Gulf of Mexico. Even though, by the treaty of peace with England, the United States extended west to the Mississippi River, the Indians who lived in the wilderness area did not accept American sovereignty. Supported by two foreign powers, England and Spain, various tribes forcefully resisted intrusions by American soldiers and settlers.

No one knows how many Indians there were in the United States at that time. According to one estimate, 849,000 Indians had lived in the area of the present United States when Europeans first arrived on the North American continent. Yet only part of that number lived in lands claimed in 1789 by the United States.

In general, the Indian population was thickest near the coasts of both the Atlantic and Pacific oceans. This meant that the original Dutch, English, and French settlers of North America had come ashore where the Indians were most numerous, which would explain why there was some fierce fighting in the early colonial days. As the eastern Indian tribes were pushed back to western New York, Pennsylvania, Ohio, Kentucky, and the western parts of Virginia, the Carolinas, and Georgia, the conflict between white settlers and Indian tribes increased.

It should be noted that the Indians were divided into hundreds of small tribes, each living independently in largely forested areas, in camps or villages near streams or other bodies of water. Meat was the basic food, with deer providing most of it, hunted with bow and arrow by men of the tribe. Women tended gardens, prepared food, and maintained households. The camps and villages were loosely organized politically, sometimes cooperating in war, sometimes not. That lack of cohesiveness made the divided Indians a relatively easy target for white penetration of their homelands.

When the new United States came into existence in 1789, the Six Nations of the Iroquois Confederation occupied most of western New York State. The Eries, Delawares, Wyandots, and the Miamis lived in western Pennsylvania and Ohio. They had been armed by the British, who had not yet yielded possession of many forts in the northern United States in hopes of maintaining control of the fur trade from which they reaped substantial profits.

In the South, the major tribes were the Cherokees, Creeks, Choctaws, Chickasaws, and Seminoles, occupying most of what is now Georgia, Alabama, Mississippi, and Florida. They cooperated with Spain, then in possession of Florida and the Louisiana Territory, including New Orleans at the mouth of the Mississippi River. Like the Indians to the north, the southern tribes fought fiercely against an ever-swelling tide of white settlers moving west to occupy their land.

It was the fixed policy of the United States government from the very beginning that no one—private individual or state—could buy land from the Indians. That was the exclusive right of the federal government. The first Congress, on July 22, 1790, passed a series of nonintercourse acts, which said, "no sale of lands made by any Indians, or any nation or tribe of Indians within the United States, shall be valid to any person or persons, or to any state . . . unless the same shall be made or duly executed at some public treaty, held under the authority of the United States."*

Despite that clear sign that the federal government intended to protect the Indians by barring whites from settling on Indian land, individual white settlers violated the law often. The relentless encroachment of the whites resulted in Indian reprisals, which in turn provoked white violence—a principal cause of the Indian wars of the period. According to Secretary of War Knox: "The desires of too many frontier white people to seize, by force or fraud, upon the neighboring Indian lands, has been, and still continues to be an unceasing cause of jealousy and hatred on the part of the Indians; and it would appear, upon a calm investigation, that until the Indians can be quieted on this point, and rely upon the protection of their lands by the United States, no well grounded hope of tranquillity can be entertained."

Clearly the federal government considered peace on the frontier a major objective. To maintain order, two means were possible. One was war against the hostile tribes to conquer them, a policy rejected by President Washington. The alternative was conciliation of the Indians by negotiation, together with payment for some of their land, guarantees of boundaries, and regulation of trade.

This policy of peace had actually been adopted even before the new government took office, and it had resulted in a series of treaties—with the Six Nations at Fort Stanwix in 1784, and with the Cherokees, Choctaws, and Chickasaws in the Treaties of Hopewell in 1785 and 1786. After Washington's inauguration, only the Creeks, one of the strongest and

---

*Those laws have been used in recent years, and are still being used, as the basis for Indian claims to regain land taken from them in the early days of the United States.

most important of the Indian nations, had not signed a formal agreement.

Taking advantage of their strategic position in the South, the Creeks had tried to maintain their land by playing off three elements: The state of Georgia, which was attempting to obtain more land for more settlers; Spain, which backed the Indians with arms and money to bolster Spanish claims to the southeastern United States; and the new United States government, which was trying to maintain peace in the South while facing war in the Northwest.

Following the 1789 confrontation between President Washington and the Senate, a group of American commissioners armed with treaty-making instructions went south to meet the Creeks at Rock Landing on the Oconee River in central Georgia. The Americans found two thousand Creek warriors gathered there, led by a most unlikely Indian chief. In the language of his people, he was called Hoboi-Hili-Moko, the Good Child King, but to historians today he is Alexander McGillivray. Born in 1759, he was the son of a Scottish trader, and his mother belonged to a powerful Creek family.

When he was fourteen years old, the boy went off to school in Charleston, studying Latin, Greek, English history, and literature. At the outbreak of the American Revolution, though, he was back with the Creeks, honored as a chief because of his mother's position in the tribe. At the age of only seventeen he was commissioned a colonel in the British Army, a step taken by the British to maintain the loyalty of the Creeks.

But at the end of the war, the Creeks were abandoned by the British, who signed away the Indians' territory without their consent to the new American government. As a result, the Indians faced a crisis. From the Carolinas and Georgia,

Alexander McGillivray wrote his first letter as leader of the Creek Indians on March 10, 1783, asking the Spanish forces occupying Pensacola to release a trader whom they had detained. The letter is signed "Alex. McGillivray, A native of & cheif [sic] of the Creek Nations." *Archivo General de Indias, Papeles de Cuba, Seville.*

land-hungry Americans were pushing relentlessly westward into the heart of the Creek nation, provoking violence and armed conflict.

For the next ten years, from 1783 until his death in 1793, McGillivray displayed remarkable talents as leader of his people. He was not a warrior and did not like fighting, leaving military operations to other chiefs. But he was a gifted diplomat, able to balance the conflicting forces affecting his nation so well that one historian compared him to Talleyrand, the famous French diplomat.

A man with piercing eyes and a grave expression, McGillivray suffered from rheumatism so severely that sometimes he could not even mount a horse. Despite his ailments and his youth, he acquired power by cementing a working relationship with the Spanish. As a result, he received arms and other supplies from them, putting the Creeks in a strong position to resist the Americans in Georgia.

When the American commissioners arrived at Rock Landing in September of 1789, they were greeted with courtesy, but they were unable to gain the land concessions from the Creeks that Georgia wanted. After that failure, Washington undertook one more effort toward a peaceful solution—by inviting McGillivray to a conference in New York in the spring of 1790.

A cavalcade of twenty-six Indian dignitaries riding in wagons and four on horseback traveled northward, receiving a dignified welcome everywhere. In New York, McGillivray and his companions were ceremoniously escorted up Wall Street to the City Tavern, where Governor Clinton and Secretary Knox were their hosts at dinner.

The next day the negotiations started, with both sides demonstrating a willingness to compromise. McGillivray yielded that part of Creek lands on which Georgians had already settled but refused to give up all the land demanded by Georgia. He also agreed to American sovereignty over lands that were within the limits of the United States but won a guarantee of protection for the homeland of the Creek Nation, a guarantee that unfortunately proved worthless during ensuing decades of relentless pressure by westbound settlers. In a secret protocol to the treaty, McGillivray even received a commission as a brigadier general in the United States Army, with a salary of $1,200 a year.

The Treaty of New York was signed on August 13, 1790, but the peace it promised lasted only briefly. After McGillivray died in 1793 at the age of thirty-four, border difficulties and sporadic warfare increased. Gradually pushed back by settlers moving in, the Creeks yielded their land piece by piece in return for promises of protection by the government—promises that were not kept.

For President Washington, though, the Treaty of New York was a welcome, if temporary, solution to the Indian problem in the South. He could now turn his attention to the more pressing threat of the Indians in the Northwest, who were much more dangerous because they were actively supported—with arms—by the British.

The Northwest crisis had grown increasingly serious as waves of white settlers descended on the territory. In April of 1788, a barge christened "the Mayflower" floated down the Ohio River. The New Englanders aboard it established Marietta as the first permanent settlement in the Northwest Territory. Soon after, a small settlement was made at Cincinnati. Later that same year, an army officer reported that "181 boats, 406 souls, 1,588 horses, 314 horned cattle, 223 sheep and 92 wagons" had passed his post in six weeks, reflecting what he called "the amazing increase" in the westward movement.

No wonder the Indians who lived in the area reacted violently. To them, the lands north of the Ohio River were home. But the Americans doggedly insisted on settling on those same fertile lands. Thus the issue was joined at a time when the military forces of the United States were insufficient to maintain the peace.

The army of the United States consisted then of only one regiment of troops, mainly because many Americans feared the consequences of maintaining a large standing army. For those who had been British subjects and who had fought the Revolutionary War, a standing army seemed a threat to liberty and republican institutions. They looked upon local militia—citizen soldiers organized by the individual states—as the bulwark of a free nation.

When Henry Knox became secretary of war in 1789, the War Department consisted of himself, one clerk, and fewer than a thousand fighting men. Knox wrote to the president estimating that it would take an army of 2,500 men and expenditures of $200,000 to crush the hostile Indians of the Northwest. It would be better, he said, to treat with the Indians on a friendly basis, at a cost he estimated at $15,000 a year. That, he added, not only would be cheaper but would absolve the United States from "blood and injustice which would stain the character of the nation."

Knox was right, as events showed. Still, when reports of Indian atrocities poured into New York, the pressures for war became too great to resist. A combined army of 1,400 regular soldiers and members of the militia set forth from Marietta under the command of Brigadier General Josiah Harmar on October 21, 1790, to attack the Miami Indians.

The result was a disaster. Supposedly experienced troops proved to be careless, while the untrained militia panicked and fled. Of the 330 regulars, 75 were killed; of the militia, 108 men died. Most of the expedition's equipment was lost or destroyed, and its horses were killed or stolen. The long-term results were worse because the Indians, instead of being forced to retreat, were encouraged by their success.

But Congress determined to strike again, voting funds to organize another regiment of infantry and authorizing the president to call out more militia. The governor of the Northwest Territory, Arthur St. Clair, who had a military background, was given command, with the rank of major general. His instructions were explicit: To send out emissaries of peace, but if that attempt failed, to attack the Indians.

Late in 1791, St. Clair started slowly north from Cincinnati, but his troops encountered miserable weather—steady rain, hail, and snow. St. Clair himself fell so sick that he had to be carried on a litter. By November 3, the army was about a hundred miles north of its starting point, on the banks of the Wabash River. Despite signs that Indians were nearby, no defense was mounted.

At sunrise on the morning of November 4, the Indians, led by their chief, Little Turtle, attacked. Advancing from tree to tree until they were in sight of the American force, they singled out the officers in their bright uniforms for their fire and left the badly trained militia leaderless. The Americans panicked.

St. Clair ordered a series of charges so that his men could retreat in an orderly fashion. But the defeated men threw away guns and packs and even abandoned the wounded in their haste to escape southward. The cost in lives was high: Thirty-five officers killed along with 588 men. One survivor reported, "I saw Captain Smith just after he was scalped, sitting on his backside, his head smoking like a chimney." Another officer wrote that the defeat would "blacken a full page in the future annals of America."

This second national military disaster in the Northwest led to a congressional investigating committee—the first one in American history. Even though the committee found him not responsible for the defeat, St. Clair resigned his commission. The committee blamed delays in the campaign, neglect in obtaining supplies, and "the want of discipline and experience in the troops."

Congress acted to remedy these defects by authorizing an additional three regiments of troops, each consisting of 980 men. Washington exercised great care in his selection of a new commanding officer, finally choosing a Revolutionary War veteran, Anthony Wayne. An impetuous and hotheaded man, Wayne had come to be known as "Mad Anthony," but in the new campaign, he was far from rash.

Making Pittsburgh his headquarters, he started to transform the raw material he had been sent into trained fighting men. Resorting to extreme measures to maintain discipline, he held courts-martial that condemned three men to death for desertion and others to be branded or whipped. It took a year—until the spring of 1794—before he felt satisfied with his force.

This time the Indians, supported by the British who still maintained forts in northern Ohio, were overconfident. General Wayne easily led his army, 3,500 strong, on a long march into the Indian territory, following the northern bank of the Maumee River. In front of them, the Indian defenses were weak.

On the morning of August 20, the Indians occupied a rude sort of stockade made from fallen trees uprooted by a tornado many years earlier. More than 1,500 Indians—the Miamis under Chief Little Turtle, the Shawnees under Black Wolf, some Ottawas, Chippewas, and Potawatomis under Blue Jacket, as well as some Sauks, Foxes, and Iroquois— waited behind the stockade.

A squadron of Wayne's dragoons charged the Indian left flank, the troopers jumping over piles of fallen timbers. On the other side, American infantrymen, with bayonets fixed, charged. The Indians fled. Within forty-five minutes, Anthony Wayne had won a great victory at the Battle of Fallen Timbers, close to where Toledo, Ohio, is today. He followed up by destroying Indian villages and burning their ripening cornfields so that they could not return, before he went into winter quarters.

Stunned by their defeat, the Indians of the Great Lakes, the Upper Mississippi, and Ohio negotiated with Wayne for six weeks before agreeing to a peace treaty. In the Treaty of Greenville, signed on August 3, 1795, the Indians yielded two-thirds of Ohio and a small piece of Indiana, opening up about 25,000 square miles of territory to the white settlers. In return, the Indians received an annuity amounting to about $10,000 a year.

Despite the treaty, however, peace did not really come to the Northwest Territory until the British withdrew from the forts they were occupying there, as we shall see in the next chapter.

13

Crisis in Foreign Affairs

PREPARING FOR HIS SECOND INAUGURATION as president on March 4, 1793, George Washington was a deeply troubled man. Now sixty-one years old, he felt gratified by the progress the new nation had made in its first four years of existence and by the fact that he had been reelected unanimously. But everywhere he looked he saw growing problems. His cabinet was feuding, Indians were fighting settlers in the Northwest and the South, and, furthermore, a foreign war was threatening the United States.

Just before noon on Inauguration Day, Washington left his Philadelphia home alone in his carriage, drawn by six white horses, and drove the short distance to Congress Hall. Precisely at noon, he entered the crowded Senate chamber to the applause of members of both Houses, the Supreme Court, foreign ministers, and invited guests. Contrary to the custom today, he made his inaugural address before taking the oath of office.

It was a short speech, the shortest inaugural address ever

given by a president of the United States, just 135 words long. Washington said:

> Fellow Citizens: I am again called upon by the voice of my country to execute the functions of its Chief Magistrate. When the occasion proper for it shall arrive, I shall endeavor to express the high sense I entertain of this distinguished honor, and of the confidence which has been reposed in me by the people of united America. Previous to the execution of any official act of the President the Constitution requires an oath of office. That oath I am now about to take, and in your presence. That if it shall be found during my administration of the Government I have in any instance violated willingly or knowingly the injunctions thereof, I may (besides incurring constitutional punishment) be subject to the upbraidings of all who are now witnesses of the present solemn ceremony.

Following that allusion to what he considered to be unfounded criticism of his administration, Washington took the oath of office administered by Supreme Court Justice William Cushing. Then he returned quietly to the presidential mansion and the major problem of the day—relations with France.

Washington's second term opened in the shadow of the French Revolution. At first, most Americans had hailed France's overthrow of the monarchy as a step toward freedom, just as the American Revolution had been. But American opinion became increasingly divided by news of violent street riots in Paris, of the execution of King Louis XVI and his frivolous queen, Marie Antoinette, and of mass beheadings by guillotine in what became known as the Reign of Terror.

Even though those events were taking place three thousand miles away across the broad Atlantic Ocean, they had a

profound effect on American politics. The Democratic-
Republicans, led by Thomas Jefferson, believed that the
French Revolution, despite its excesses, would end in order
and liberty. But to the Federalists, led by Alexander
Hamilton, the French Revolution seemed a horrifying exam-
ple of the dangers of anarchy, irreligion, and mob rule.

At a time when political passions ran high, the deep division within the nation was reflected in the personal jour-
nalism of the day. The Jeffersonians were branded "Gallic
jackals" or "frog-eating, man-eating, blood-drinking can-
nibals." In return, they called the Hamiltonians "British
bootlickers."

Only a month after Washington's second inauguration, the
French Revolution became the most important issue facing
the nation—because France not only proclaimed itself a republic and declared war on Great Britain and other European nations, but it also appointed Edmond Genêt as its
minister to the United States. By going to war with England,
France raised the issue of American aid under the Treaty of
Alliance of 1778. France had helped the United States to win
its independence from England. Would America now help
France?

At nine o'clock on the morning of April 19, the cabinet
met in Washington's office to consider America's course of
action. Present were Secretary of State Jefferson, Secretary
of the Treasury Hamilton, Secretary of War Knox, and Attorney General Edmund Randolph.

The president opened the meeting by posing a pressing
question: Should the United States remain neutral?

Hamilton, Knox, and Randolph favored a forthright proclamation of neutrality. Jefferson, who said he opposed entering the war as much as anyone, added that the United States

was in a strong position to obtain concessions from England in return for neutrality.

Washington's next questions proved to be more controversial: Should the minister of France be received? And if so, how?

Hamilton opposed recognition of the new French government. He withdrew his objections, though, following Jefferson's argument that the United States had already recognized France when Gouverneur Morris, the American representative in Paris, appeared before the French National Assembly.

Did that mean that the United States felt itself bound by the Treaty of Alliance of 1778?

For Hamilton, who favored the British over the French, renunciation of the treaty was essential to preserve American neutrality. Knox, who almost always followed Hamilton's lead, supported him. But Jefferson's dissent raised a compelling point. He insisted that the treaty was valid because treaties are made between nations, not governments. Randolph, who usually considered himself independent, supported Jefferson. President Washington himself decided that the United States should adopt a policy of neutrality and pursue "a conduct friendly and impartial toward the belligerent powers."

Washington issued his proclamation on April 22, 1793. It prohibited American citizens from "aiding or abetting hostilities," but doing so was easier said than done. The difficulty stemmed largely from the activities of one man, the new French minister to the United States. Edmond Charles Edouard Genêt, called Citizen Genêt in the style of the French Revolution, was only thirty years old at the time he arrived in the United States. Almost immediately, he became a great storm center, having a profound effect on

American politics and foreign relations because of his personality no less than his politics.

Genêt had a most unlikely background for a representative of revolutionary France. Born in the shadow of King Louis XVI's palace at Versailles, he had been educated under the direction of his father, an interpreter at the foreign ministry. His oldest sister served as first lady-in-waiting to Queen Marie Antoinette. He learned many languages, including English, from his tutors and, in 1781, succeeded his father as an official in the foreign ministry. After a tour of duty as a diplomat in Russia, he returned to Paris—and enthusiastically changed his allegiance, siding with the new leadership of the French Revolution. Following the execution of the king and the declaration of war against England, the former aristocrat was sent to the United States to win its support in the war, landing in Charleston on April 8, 1793.

A rash young man who regarded the normal diplomatic traits of caution and discretion as almost treasonable to the revolution, Genêt instantly began trying to convert the United States into a military base of operations for France. He issued warrants for privateers—privately owned ships— to prey upon British shipping. He also sought to enlist American fighting men for expeditions against Florida, Louisiana, and Canada.

Everywhere he went on his travels north from Charleston to the capital in Philadelphia, Citizen Genêt was greeted with speeches, fireworks, feasts, and toasts. His triumphal welcome convinced him that the American people were firmly committed to the cause of France. "The real Americans are wild with joy," Genêt wrote back to France in a diplomatic report. Still, he had not yet presented his credentials to President Washington. That important event took place at 2 P.M. on Saturday, May 18.

It was a curious encounter. The tone was set when Genêt saw a bust of King Louis XVI in the president's parlor. Although the piece of sculpture was not meant as a signal, to Genêt it seemed clear that his formal reception by the president would be different from the warm ovations he had received from the people.

It was. On one hand, there was the handsome young Genêt—a man of medium stature, with a broad brow, auburn hair, and a courtly appearance. On the other, there was Washington, twice his age, stately, dignified, and determined not to be charmed by the young Frenchman or deterred from his policy of neutrality.

Secretary of State Jefferson formally introduced the new minister to Washington. Genêt stepped forward and presented his written credentials. Washington received them, thus acknowledging Genêt as France's official representative to the United States, but there were no words of welcome.

"Old man Washington can't forgive my success," Genêt wrote home. But he made the mistake that many others have made since—he mistook the applause of curious crowds for approval. Still, the crowds certainly did approve when American-owned privateers raised the tricolor flag of France on British merchant ships they had captured in the Atlantic and brought into American ports. Altogether, Genêt commissioned twelve privateers, which captured more than eighty British ships before he was finished—all of this despite strong objections by the British minister in Philadelphia.

Nevertheless, Genêt's machinations eventually undid him. In July, word spread that a captured British merchant ship, the *Little Sarah*, had been renamed the *Petite Democrate*. Even though the Washington administration had ordered ships commissioned by Genêt to stay out of American waters, the vessel was being armed in Delaware Bay. When Jefferson warned Genêt to cease violating American neutrality, the self-confident Frenchman insisted that the ship would go to sea as planned. Without a navy, the United States had no means of stopping it.

So the *Petite Democrate* sailed—but Genêt had destroyed his mission to enlist the United States as an ally of France. He had alienated even Jefferson, who had been one of his strongest supporters, along with many others. Jefferson described Genêt as "hot headed, all imagination, no judgement, passionate, disrespectful and even indecent towards the President."

Washington himself was furious. He wrote to Jefferson: "Is the Minister of the French Republic to set the acts of this Government with impunity? And then threaten the Executive with an appeal to the people? What must the world think of such conduct, and of the Government of the United States in submitting to it?"

A cabinet meeting followed, and the American government decided to ask France to recall the impetuous minister. At the same time, the United States recalled its own minister to France, Gouverneur Morris, whose relations with the French Government had become strained.

By an ironic twist, Genêt found himself in danger at home, too. During his absence, his party, the moderate Giroi. ists, had been swept out of power by the radical Jacobins. As a Girondist, Genêt was declared to be a public enemy and ordered to return to France. It became clear to him that if he did so he would answer for his "crimes" by having his head chopped off on the guillotine.

Instead of going back to France, Genêt asked for—and received—asylum in the United States. Ready now to settle down peaceably, he married a daughter of Governor Clinton of New York and retired to the life of a country gentleman in the Hudson Valley, where he remained without further controversy until he died in 1836.

With the Genêt problem solved, the United States still faced serious difficulties as it tried to remain neutral in the war between England and France. During 1793, both sides repeatedly seized American ships and their cargoes to prevent the other from receiving food or supplies. In the French port of Bordeaux alone, soon there were eighty American ships being held and illegally forbidden to sail.

But the French abuses against American ships were minor compared to British actions. On November 6, 1793, the British secretly issued an order authorizing the capture of all neutral ships carrying provisions to and from the French West Indies. Under that order, the British Navy eventually captured a total of 250 American merchant ships.

Equally important for strained Anglo-American relations was a residue from the peace treaty of 1783. Despite having agreed in that treaty to surrender its inland forts, England still occupied eight within the geographical limits of the United States and refused to give them up. Two, at Dutchman's Point and Pointe-au-Fer, secured the outlet from Lake Champlain. Three, at Oswegatchie, Oswego, and Niagara, controlled navigation on the Saint Lawrence River. Another, Fort Erie, was at the eastern end of Lake Erie. Detroit controlled the strip between Lakes Erie and Huron. The small fortified island of Michilmacinack, at the tip of the Michigan peninsula, controlled the entrance to three lakes, Huron, Michigan, and Superior.

Behind England's refusal to give up the forts was the fur trade, at that time the largest and most profitable industry in the United States. From the Great Lakes to the Saint Lawrence River and then across the Atlantic, a steady stream of

During his second term as president, George Washington was constrained to ask France to recall Edmond Charles Genêt, its minister to the United States. Portrait by Ezra Ames. *Gift of Mrs. George C. Genêt, Collection of the Albany Institute of History and Art.*

beaver furs, trapped mostly by Indians, went to supply the demand of fashionable Europeans for hats and other attire. The fur trade furnished huge profits for Montreal traders, English shippers, and London importers.

Another factor also had a great bearing on the relationship between Britain and its former colonies during that period. Despite its political independence, the United States remained very much connected with its former ruler economically. Early in the 1790s, the United States was the largest foreign customer of English trade, taking at least one-fifth of all English manufactures. Important as the American trade was for British prosperity, it was vital for the national existence of the United States. Ninety percent of American imports came from Great Britain, and much of the revenue of the new American government came from its tariff on imports. Obviously, both sides had strong reasons to maintain friendly trading relations.

The British kept jeopardizing those relations, however, by their seizures of American ships as well as by their policy of holding on to the western forts and arming hostile Indians. These British actions produced a political split within the United States. The Democratic-Republicans hotly called for retaliatory measures against England, even "a second war of independence" if necessary. On the other hand, the Federalists, while critical of the British, believed that war would split the country, and urged Washington to send a special envoy to England as a last resort to preserve peace.

For that important mission, Washington chose his old friend and supporter John Jay, the chief justice of the United States. Then forty-eight years old, Jay was well equipped for undertaking sensitive diplomatic negotiations. During the American Revolution, he had been a minister to Spain. Then he had helped negotiate the treaty of peace that ended the war in 1783. He had served as secretary for foreign affairs of the United States until Jefferson took over as secretary of state in 1790.

In appointing Jay, President Washington noted: "My objects are to prevent war, if justice can be obtained by fair and strong representations of the injuries which this country has sustained from Great Britain." Specifically, Jay's instructions were to secure British evacuation of the western forts, to obtain reparation for British seizure of American ships, and to negotiate a commercial treaty. Yet he was warned against making any agreement contrary to the country's treaty with France or that did not allow American ships to trade with the British West Indies.

Jay arrived in England on June 12, 1794, and immediately began official conversations under far from favorable conditions. It was as if he had been told to play a game in which the British held all the cards. Their navy controlled the seas, while the United States had no navy. Jay could hardly help recalling that Hamilton had said it seemed vain to believe that the British, "fortified by the alliances of the greatest part of Europe, will submit to our demands." Nevertheless, the British received the new American envoy cordially, wined and dined him, and catered to his vanity by appearing to regard him as an important personage.

For months, though, the negotiations yielded no major English concessions. Finally, on November 19, with Jay convinced that he could get no better terms, he signed the treaty that still bears his name—a treaty that destroyed his national political future and caused a storm of political protests in the United States.

Looking back, it is hard to see why the Jay Treaty aroused such a furor. Jay actually obtained two of the prime objects of his mission—a British promise to evacuate the Northwest

Territory forts by 1796, and a limited right of American ships to trade with the British West Indies. He failed, however, to obtain British acceptance of freedom of the seas for neutral vessels, and the British refused to give up their rights to "impress" seamen—that is, to take by force from the crews of American vessels persons who they claimed were British subjects. Jay also agreed that molasses, sugar, coffee, cocoa, and cotton carried by American ships from the British West Indies would not be transported to any place but the United States.

When news of the treaty's provisions reached the United States early in 1795, Jay was burned in effigy so often that he remarked that he could find his way across the country by the light of the flames. At a meeting in New York, Hamilton was pelted by stones when he tried to speak in favor of the treaty. In South Carolina, copies of the treaty were set aflame and calls were made for Jay's impeachment. Even Washington himself was the subject of bitter criticism because of the treaty.

In Washington's mind, though, the basic consideration was that the treaty would guarantee peace with Britain, averting the prospect of another war. So, despite the fact that he questioned some of its provisions, he submitted it to the Senate for ratification. On a straight party vote, the Federalist majority approved the treaty on June 24—by exactly the two-thirds majority required, twenty for the treaty, ten against.

By signing the treaty, Washington did not end the controversy. Democratic-Republican opponents of the treaty attempted to kill it in the House of Representatives by a devious measure. They demanded that Washington turn over papers relating to the Jay Treaty, contending that the House had the power to investigate such documents. Washington refused, citing the Constitution's provision that treaties ratified by the Senate and signed by the president were the supreme law of the land, and he said that the House had no role in treaty-making.

Although the Jay Treaty met so much opposition in its time, it proved to be a major step forward in the growth of the United States. According to the noted historian Samuel Eliot Morison: ". . . It preserved the peace, secured America's territorial integrity, and established a base for western expansion."

Another by-product of the Jay Treaty was the successful conclusion of negotiations with Spain involving two controversial issues causing much concern in the American South and West. In 1795, Thomas Pinckney, then the American minister to England, was dispatched to Spain because that country, an ally of Britain in the war against France, had decided to pull out and make a separate peace. In doing so, Spain wanted to make sure of America's friendship.

Thus Pinckney was able to obtain all the United States desired—a grant of navigation rights on the Mississippi plus rights to deposit American goods in New Orleans, along with Spanish agreement that the southern border of the United States was at the thirty-first parallel, not at the Ohio River as Spain had claimed before. A treaty including those important concessions was signed on October 27, 1795, at San Lorenzo, a mountain village in Spain, and since then it has been known as either the Treaty of San Lorenzo or Pinckney's Treaty.

Following its adoption, one major foreign problem continued to face the United States: What could it do to stop the Barbary pirates from capturing and enslaving American seamen?

14

The Barbary Pirates

"MILLIONS FOR DEFENSE, but not one cent for tribute!"

That patriotic slogan inspired American hearts in the early years of the United States, but it wasn't really true. For years, the government had been paying tribute to the Barbary States of North Africa to protect American ships in the Mediterranean Sea or to ransom American sailors captured by the pirates from those states. The reason was that the young United States had no navy to protect its far-flung commerce.

After the treaty of peace ending the Revolutionary War, American foreign trade had grown rapidly, tripling in volume between 1789 and 1797. This trade was largely carried on by ships built in the United States and manned by American crews. The merchant ships had to depend on themselves, though, or the friendly navies of other nations, for protection on the high seas. The last American warship had been sold in 1785, two years before the adoption of the Constitution, when the weak government operating under the

Articles of Confederation had decided that it was just too expensive to maintain a navy.

As a result, pirates in the Mediterranean learned that the stars and stripes of the United States represented a powerless new nation unable to retaliate if its ships were seized. Along the coast of North Africa, piracy had become a way of life because it provided an opportunity for acquiring wealth quickly—merely by capturing unarmed merchant ships and confiscating their cargoes. Moreover, the pirates demanded and received additional money as ransom for captured seamen. Some other seagoing nations also considered paying the blackmail the cheapest and easiest way of avoiding trouble.

Situated on the North African coast, the Barbary States—Morocco, Tunisia, Algiers, and Tripoli—controlled commerce throughout the Mediterranean Sea. While Morocco was independent, the other three owed allegiance to the sultan of Turkey on the far eastern shores of the Mediterranean. Because of the distance involved, though, they operated without restraint from the sultan as long as they supplied revenue for the Turks. The Moslem Turks, who regarded Christians as infidels, considered all infidel ships fair game for them.

America's serious concern with the pirates dated back to July 25, 1785, when the schooner *Maria* from Boston had been captured off Cape Saint Vincent by an Algerian warship of fourteen guns. Five days later, the *Dauphin* out of Philadelphia had been captured near Lisbon. Both vessels, with their crews, were escorted into Algiers, where twenty-one captured American seamen were stripped of their clothes and given filthy rags to wear, then put to various kinds of slave labor—as sweepers, gardeners, or even lion keepers. One captive went insane and died in a dungeon. Several others died of the bubonic plague. The survivors were to remain as prisoners for twelve years before being ransomed.

It was a different story when the brig *Betsy* was captured by a corsair out of Morocco at about the same time. Sidi Mohamet, the emperor of Morocco, vowed friendship for the United States but held the crew as hostages until a treaty between the two countries was negotiated. Under that treaty, signed in 1787, Morocco agreed to permit American ships to pass unmolested in return for a payment of $10,000 a year. But the pirates of Algiers, Tunisia, and Tripoli continued their marauding without much interference for the next several years.

In 1793, eleven American ships were captured during October and November and carried into Algiers, with one hundred and eleven officers and men made prisoner. One of them, John Foss, a sailor on the brig *Polly* of Newburyport, managed to write a graphic account of their treatment by the pirates:

> They immediately hoisted out a large launch and about one hundred of the pirates jumped on board, all armed, some with Scimitres and pistols, others with pikes, spears, lances, knives, etc. . . . As soon as they came aboard our vessel, they made signs for us all to go forward, assuring us in several languages that if we did not obey their commands, they would immediately massacre us all. They then went below into the cabin, steerage and every place they could get below deck and broke open all the Trunks and Chests there, clothing, books, Charts, Quadrants and every moveable article that did not consist of Cargo or furniture. Then they came back on deck and stripped the cloathes off our backs, all except a shirt and a pair of drawers.

The prisoners were taken through the streets of Algiers to the palace of the ruler, called the dey of Algiers. The dey told them he had proposed a treaty of peace with the United States, but had not received a satisfactory answer. Annoyed at what he considered to be a rejection of his peaceful overtures, he added, "Now I have got you, you Christian dogs, you shall eat stones."

The dey picked out four of the younger men to be his personal slaves and sent the rest to foul-smelling dungeons where, Foss later reported, they found several other Americans and about six hundred Christian slaves of various nationalities "with wretched habits, dejected contenances and chains on their legs."

On the day after their arrival, the new captives were shackled with chains weighing more than twenty-five pounds fastened to their ankles. Many of the prisoners were forced to work at blasting huge rocks in quarries. Teams of other prisoners then pulled sleds bearing blocks of stone, some weighing up to forty tons, down to the harbor, where they were dumped to strengthen a breakwater.

Despite the dey's complaint about the lack of American action on the piracy issue, at least one step had been taken. In 1787, the United States had employed an agent in Paris to try to obtain the release of its captured citizens by paying no more than $200 per captive, but the dey asked for almost $3,000 a man. Over the next few years, while more than a dozen captives languished in prison, the negotiations broke down. Finally, in 1790, Washington and Jefferson decided that Congress must deal with the problem. Jefferson told the lawmakers: "It rests with Congress to decide between war, tribute and ransom as the means of re-establishing our Mediterranean commerce."

Without a navy, however, the United States had little choice. After a letter arrived from the captives threatening to abandon Christ and country if something were not done to help them, Congress appropriated $54,000 to ransom them—amounting to about $2,000 a prisoner. John Paul Jones, the admiral of Revolutionary War fame, was assigned to obtain their release, but he died before he could carry out his mission. And so the captives remained as slaves.

It was not until 1794 that effective action was taken. By a narrow vote, Congress at last decided that a navy was necessary and authorized the construction of six frigates of the finest quality to be manned by fifty-four officers and two thousand sailors. The job of turning the congressional mandate into reality was given to Henry Knox, the secretary of war, who recruited two well-known naval architects and shipbuilders, Joshua Humphreys and Josiah Fox.

Ironically, Humphreys, who designed the vessels that would become the most famous warships in American history, was a peace-loving Quaker from Haverford, Pennsylvania. Apprenticed to a ship's carpenter as a youth, he had later started his own business and built many ships during the Revolutionary War. In 1794, Humphreys capped his career by supplying the ideas for the new American fleet— while Fox did the actual drafting of the plans. Those plans resulted in the construction of vessels named the *United States*, the *Constitution*, the *President*, the *Constellation*, the *Chesapeake*, and the *Congress*, all destined to become household words in the War of 1812. For his work on those historic ships, Humphreys has been called "the father of the American navy."

While the ships were being built, two American envoys crossed the Atlantic Ocean to make another effort toward obtaining the release of the prisoners peaceably. The negotiations were conducted by a remarkable team of poet-diplomats who had been classmates at Yale—Joel Barlow and David Humphreys (no relative of Joshua, the shipbuilder).

David Humphreys had been a secretary to President Washington but had also served as minister to Portugal. He wrote satirical poetry and was a member of the select literary clique known as the Hartford Wits, as was Barlow.

Humphreys went to Paris to enlist the aid of the French in getting the prisoners released while Barlow went directly to Algiers. There, negotiations had already been started by the American consul, Joseph Donaldson, Jr. By then, word that a United States fleet was under construction had reached Algiers, and the dey was becoming more amenable to an agreement.

Friendly as the dey now appeared to be, he still insisted on a substantial ransom. He signed a treaty on September 5, 1795, in which he agreed to set free all his American captives for $642,500 in cash, plus an annual payment of $21,600 in naval stores, and an additional $36,000 worth of supplies like damask, jewelry, linens, and broadcloth. The Senate ratified the treaty early in 1796, and the American captives, now reduced to sixty-five, returned home in the spring of 1797.

Having restored friendly relations with Algiers, the most powerful of the Barbary states, the American government started a new round of negotiations with Tunisia and Tripoli. On November 4, 1796, Barlow concluded a treaty with Tripoli after agreeing to pay the comparatively small sum of $58,000 as tribute. It took a little longer to reach agreement with Tunisia. After the United States agreed to pay the dey of Tunisia $107,000, a treaty was signed on August 17, 1797.

Still, these treaties did not end American troubles with the Barbary pirates. For years, the United States kept making payments of gold and tribute in the form of naval supplies to the Barbary States, while only an uncertain peace reigned in the Mediterranean. The United States, in effect, was buying time until its new navy could sail forth to defend American shipping from piracy.

It wasn't until 1798, when John Adams was the president, that three of America's warships, the *Constitution*, the *United States*, and the *Constellation*, were ready for sea. In that same year, Congress established a separate Department of the Navy. Before then, naval functions had been assigned to the secretaries of war and the treasury.

Yet it took a long time for the navy to humble the troublesome Barbary pirates. The main reason was that the United States and its warships became involved, first, in an undeclared war at sea with France in the late 1790s and, later, in the War of 1812 with the British.

Not until the end of that war did the United States direct major attention to the problem of the Barbary pirates. In 1815, two squadrons of American warships sailed into the Mediterranean, commanded by Commodore William Bainbridge and Commodore Stephen Decatur, veterans of the War of 1812. Decatur is remembered today mostly for his famous toast, given at a dinner in his honor: "Our country! In her intercourse with foreign nations, may she always be right; but our country, right or wrong."

That display of American naval might and the capture of some Algerian ships caused the pirate leaders to capitulate. They signed treaties abolishing the tribute and released all remaining American prisoners. After almost thirty years of humiliation, at last the United States had made the Mediterranean Sea safe for American merchant ships.

15

The Whiskey Rebellion

AT DAWN ON THE MORNING OF JULY 16, 1794, about fifty angry men carrying rifles marched to the home of General John Neville at Bower Hill, not far from the small settlement of Pittsburgh in western Pennsylvania. General Neville, who had a fine record as an officer in the Revolutionary War, was one of the most popular men in Monongahela County. But he had just been appointed regional supervisor for the collection of a new federal excise tax on whiskey—and that made him a target for the irate farmers of the area.

One day earlier, he and a United States marshal had traveled through the county serving summonses on local distillers, most of them farmers, who had refused to pay the hated new tax. The official notices ordered them to "put aside all manner of business and excuses" and appear in August, the height of the harvest season, before a judge in Philadelphia, some three hundred miles eastward across the rugged Pennsylvania mountains.

As if that were not sufficiently upsetting, somehow a

rumor spread that the delinquent taxpayers would be dragged off to Philadelphia by force. To the proud individualists of the backwoods outpost, it seemed that their rights as American citizens were being violated. Furious, they assembled outside General Neville's imposing house, the finest in the neighborhood.

Neville ordered the armed throng to stand back. Then he fired a shot, wounding one of the men, who later died. At the general's signal, a round of fire from his slaves wounded five more of the attackers. The mob dispersed but the next day a larger group appeared, bolstered by members of the local militia. By coincidence, the militia had been called up in answer to President Washington's request for troops to fight Indians, but they were ready to support their neighbors.

Late in the afternoon, the militia began to parade in front of General Neville's house, now protected by ten soldiers from nearby Fort Pitt. The commander of the militia, James McFarlane, a veteran of the Revolutionary War, demanded the surrender of Neville. The soldiers replied that he had already left the area. McFarlane demanded that the soldiers depart, too. They refused—and shots broke out.

At one point during the confusion, McFarlane heard a shout from the house and, thinking it was a call for a truce, stepped out from behind a tree to answer it. He fell under a hail of bullets. Outraged, the militiamen set fire to the house and its outbuildings, forcing the soldiers to surrender. Although nobody can be sure about the actual number of casualties, it is believed that two or three persons were killed and several wounded during the skirmish at Bower Hill.

That marked the start of the Whiskey Rebellion, the first major domestic test of the new federal government. Throughout the West, reaction to the excise tax followed the tradition of the American colonists who had protested the British taxes on stamps and tea back in the 1770s. But now the opposition was more complicated politically.

Like Shays' Rebellion in western Massachusetts as recently as 1786, the Whiskey Rebellion illustrated a conflict of interests among different groups of Americans themselves. To those who lived along the Atlantic seaboard, Secretary of the Treasury Hamilton's idea of a tax on distilled spirits seemed perfectly reasonable. Inland, though, whiskey was more than just a potent drink. In an era of poor roads, farmers converted their surplus rye and corn into whiskey—twenty-four bushels of rye could be made into sixteen gallons of whiskey—because the smaller amounts of liquor were much easier to transport.

So the pioneer families of the West used whiskey as a form of currency, to buy necessities that could not be produced locally, and even some ministers were paid in "Monongahela rye." Every fall, a packhorse train carrying whiskey and furs went east over the rugged mountains to be traded for salt and iron. But the tax collectors wanted to be paid in money, which was scarce on the self-sufficient frontier.

Western farming communities felt, therefore, that Hamilton's proposal was terribly unfair. Why should they pay a tax on their grain just because a distant government needed funds? Let those near the coast, whose trade benefited from the new government's policies, pay the expenses, they said. So the inevitable result was a deepening split between Hamiltonian Federalists mostly living in coastal cities and the rural Democratic-Republican societies of the interior emerging as strong supporters of Thomas Jefferson.

But the westerners were divided among themselves, too. That became apparent during a series of meetings following the Bower Hill affair. At one gathering, Hugh Henry

Brackenridge, a moderate-minded lawyer and writer from Pittsburgh, told the radical dissidents bluntly: "What had been done might be morally right, but it was legally wrong . . . it was high treason." He said that the president had the power to call out the militia against further threats and advised those who had been at Bower Hill to apply for an amnesty.

That infuriated the radicals led by David Bradford, a particularly rash lawyer. He sent out a letter proclaiming: "We have fully deliberated and have determined that with head, heart and voice, we will support the opposition to the excise tax." According to one historian, Bradford must have had delusions of grandeur, with "visions of himself as the Washington of the West, laying the foundations of a new nation."

At first, it appeared that Bradford and other leaders of the rebellion had widespread support. A meeting was called for August 1 at Braddock's Field, the site of the historic defeat of the British Army in 1755, when George Washington as a young army officer had taken part in the fighting. Nearly forty years later, about five thousand rebels, a very large number for those days, attended the protest rally.

Bradford assumed the role of major general in command. "Mounted on a superb horse in splendid trappings, arrayed in full martial uniform, with plumes floating in air and sword drawn, he rode over the grounds, gave orders to the military and harangued the multitude." So wrote Brackenridge in his account of the uprising.

The next day the protesters marched on Pittsburgh, about eight miles away, with vague intentions of destroying that seat of the local government. But Pittsburgh residents acted hospitably, distributing casks of whiskey, and the moderate elements were able to restrain the mob so that the only damage caused was one barn burned. Although the leaders of the rebellion talked boldly about independence, civil war, and possible union with Great Britain or Spain, no organized movement developed with any clearly defined goals.

But back east in Philadelphia, the national capital, news of the rebellion was taken very seriously. An outraged President Washington called a cabinet meeting—by coincidence, on August 2, the same day as the march on Pittsburgh—to consider how to preserve the Union from falling apart in the face of violence and disorder. Washington's concern went far beyond the mere collection of the excise tax. He said he was worried about anarchy if rebels were permitted to continue trampling on the law without being punished.

Hamilton held that the crisis must be met by force of arms despite the insistence of state officials that the courts were adequate to handle the task of quelling the riots. The president voiced his determination to end the rebellion by going "every length that the Constitution and laws would permit, but no further." He sought guidance from Supreme Court Justice James Wilson, who reported to him that enforcement of the laws in western Pennsylvania was being "obstructed by combinations too powerful to be suppressed" merely by the courts.

And so on August 7, Washington issued a proclamation:

It is in my judgement necessary under the circumstances of the case to take measures calling forth the militia in order to suppress the combinations aforesaid, and to cause the laws to be duly executed; and I have accordingly determined to do so, feeling the deepest regret for the occasion, but withal the most solemn conviction that the essential interests of the Union demand it, that the very existence of Government and the fundamental principles of social order are materially involved in the issue, and that the patriotism and firmness of all good citizens are seriously called upon, as occasions may require, to aid in the effectual suppression of so fatal a spirit.

Washington took two steps. First, he asked the governors of Pennsylvania, New Jersey, Virginia, and Maryland to call out thirteen thousand militiamen to put down the insurrection. But he also appointed three commissioners to go to western Pennsylvania to see if they could resolve the problem without force of arms.

In late August, the three commissioners met with a committee named by the rebels. They offered a general amnesty for crimes committed during the riots in return for restoration of order, but the rebels seemed divided. At a subsequent meeting, though, the tide turned in favor of acceptance after a two-hour speech by Albert Gallatin, a Swiss-born landowner, who later became a member of Congress and secretary of the treasury. He warned against thoughtless sedition because "illegal opposition, when reduced, has a tendency to make the people abject and the government tyrannic."

After a lengthy debate, the rebel meeting by a narrow vote accepted the commissioners' proposal. But the rebels decided to hold a public referendum on September 11 on the question: "Will the people submit to the laws of the United States upon the terms proposed by the commissioners of the United States?" Although there were a few who rejected the proposal, the overwhelming majority accepted it.

The voting came too late. No matter that it was clear by the third week of September that no organized resistance remained in western Pennsylvania, the federal army had already gone on the move. Washington and Hamilton felt convinced that a show of force was needed to end the rebellion decisively—and Washington, as an experienced soldier, realized that the army had to move before winter closed the roads and made operations impossible.

From Virginia came 3,300 troops under the command of Governor Henry Lee. Governor Thomas S. Lee of Maryland led 2,350 militiamen. New Jersey contributed 2,100 men under the command of Governor Richard Howell, and Pennsylvania's 5,200 men were led by Governor Thomas Mifflin. Altogether, the army numbered 12,950 men, but the rate of desertion was high, discipline was difficult to maintain, and sickness reduced its strength. At one time, more than half of the Pennsylvania contingent fell ill with dysentery and were unable to perform their duties. Supplying and transporting the men proved to be a difficult task as well.

The westerners had a term of scorn for the federal army—"the watermelon army." That came from a satire written by Brackenridge, in which one of his characters said: "Brothers, you may not think to frighten us . . . [with] water-melon armies from the Jersey shores; they would cut a much better figure in warring with the crabs and oysters about the Capes of Delaware."

Despite all of the difficulties, the federal army massed at Carlisle and Cumberland in preparation for the march over the mountains to Pittsburgh. President Washington, accompanied by Hamilton, arrived at Carlisle to review the troops on October 4 and was greeted by bells and salutes, although the people of the town looked on in silence.

At Carlisle, Washington received two representatives from the West, who reported that order was being restored. The troops were not needed, they said. But Washington remained determined. He told them that "nothing short of the most unequivocal proofs of absolute submission should retard the march of the army." He assured them that a spirit of revenge would not be tolerated in the army, which would act only in aid of the courts.

After reviewing additional troops in Cumberland, Washington designated Governor Lee of Virginia as commander, with Hamilton as the civilian head. Washington then returned to Philadelphia, while the army pushed west.

Heavy rains in the mountains delayed the march. According to one report: "The wagon trains were beset by almost insuperable conditions; roads muddy, rocky, and, on the mountains, dangerous; wagons breaking down; horses lame, sick and foundering, with the consequent necessity of impressing more from the reluctant inhabitants . . . Fortunate indeed were the soldiers if they did not have to retire supperless to a mud bed and spend the night with rain beating on their defenseless forms."

Finally, on October 24, the army entered Pittsburgh, accompanied by a federal judge, attorney, and marshal. The officials immediately began an investigation into the origins of the rebellion, trying to find its ringleaders.

But David Bradford had already fled farther west, and he was never captured. Despite a month of painstaking inquiry, it proved impossible to develop any solid evidence against any of the supposed leaders of the collapsed rebellion. So the expedition resulted only in the arrest of eighteen minor figures.

Starting on November 25, they were marched back across the mountains through snow and ice, each guarded by two troopers with swords drawn. Upon arriving in Philadelphia, they were charged with treason, but the lawyers defending them argued that they had been involved merely in riots. After much legal maneuvering, all except two were acquitted. One of these was judged insane, however, and the other a simpleton. Washington pardoned them both.

Thus ended the Whiskey Rebellion. Jefferson said, "An insurrection was announced and proclaimed and armed against, but never could be found." Hamilton had a different opinion. The government, he insisted, had gained "reputation and strength" by demonstrating that it could compel obedience to the laws.

Yet there were several other results. President Washington had shown that the federal government would use the army, if needed, to enforce the law. While his action set a precedent for federal law enforcement, it also showed the limits of federal authority, because most of the small distillers continued to evade the excise tax until the law was repealed in 1802.

The major impact of the Whiskey Rebellion was political. In the short run, the controversy helped the Federalists. The party regained full control of Congress in the 1794 election, but the party's influence was really waning. In 1795, Albert Gallatin, a strong Jeffersonian and a leader of the moderates during the troubles over the tax, was elected to the House of Representatives, a sure sign that the opposition party was gaining strength.

The major victim of the Whiskey Rebellion was someone who had absolutely nothing to do with it—Edmund Randolph, one of Washington's closest and most trusted advisers. Randolph had been associated with Washington ever since the days of the Constitutional Convention, when Randolph had presented the Virginia Plan that formed the basis of the new Constitution. He had been the nation's first attorney general and had been secretary of state for two years, replacing Jefferson. His job put him in daily contact with Washington, who considered him a close friend.

On the morning of August 19, 1795, Randolph as usual went to Washington's office. There, he found two other members of the cabinet—Timothy Pickering, who had succeeded Knox as secretary of war, and Oliver Wolcott, who had succeeded Hamilton as secretary of the treasury. The president greeted Randolph with unusual formality.

"Mr. Randolph," he said, "here is a letter I desire you to read, and make such explanations as you choose."

Randolph took the document and read it through in silence. It was a letter written in French by Joseph Fauchet, the French minister to the United States, describing the Whiskey Rebellion to his superiors in Paris. The letter had been captured at sea by the British and sent back to Philadelphia to cause dissension in the American government. The British minister gave the intercepted letter to Wolcott, who brought it to the attention of the president.

In the letter, Fauchet implied that the Federalists had actively provoked violence in the West as a means of destroying their political opponents. The charge rested on confidential information allegedly provided by Randolph, and it was even intimated that he had sought a bribe.

As Washington watched intently, Randolph finished reading the letter.

"I will explain what I know," Randolph said. Washington nodded.

Randolph proceeded to go through the letter paragraph by paragraph, refuting every charge. Never, he said, had he asked or received any money from Fauchet nor had he encouraged the Pennsylvania insurrection. When he finished, Washington asked him to leave the room. While the president consulted behind closed doors with the two other members of his cabinet, Randolph became increasingly angry. He felt that Washington's lack of trust in him made his own position impossible.

So Randolph wrote a letter formally resigning his post, and then resolved to prove his innocence. A few months later, he published a 103-page document called "A Vindication," but it was too late. His public career had been ruined as the result of unsubstantiated charges supported by two fierce Federalists determined to drive him from the cabinet and the ear of the president. In the words of one of Washington's biographers: "The machinations of Pickering and Wolcott in this episode violated every fundamental of fair play." Most historians believe that the idea that Randolph solicited a bribe was absurd. Why, then, did Washington believe it?

The best explanation appears to be that in the bitter political climate surrounding the Whiskey Rebellion, President Washington really feared that the republic was falling apart. But Randolph did not share Washington's conviction that force was necessary to put down the uprising. Thus, Washington must have felt that Randolph was disloyal to him personally and to the Union.

At any rate, the fact that even George Washington doubted an old friend so unjustifiably provides clear evidence of the deep political passions within the United States as his second term as president drew toward a close.

16

Farewell

AFTER THE TURBULENCE OF 1794 AND 1795—often described as the most critical years of the early United States—President Washington looked forward eagerly to retiring to the peace of his beloved Mount Vernon. He was determined that 1796 would be his last full year in office. When Alexander Hamilton asked him how he could leave if the nation were threatened, Washington replied that after March 4, 1797, "no consideration under heaven that I can foresee shall again draw me from the walks of private life."

What was the state of the nation, only seven years old, as Washington prepared to give up his post?

For one thing, it was growing rapidly. Immigrants from Europe were arriving in large numbers and pushing west. Also, the country itself had expanded—with Vermont, admitted on March 4, 1791, becoming the fourteenth state; Kentucky, on June 1, 1792, the fifteenth; and Tennessee, on June 1, 1796, the sixteenth. Ohio was attracting large numbers of settlers, too, although it did not become a state until 1803.

During its first decade, and for many years after, the United States was a nation of farmers who produced food not only for their families but for export. In New York, as just one example, wheat was raised in large quantities for shipment to Europe, where the essential grain was desperately needed because of the wars that had hurt agriculture there. From the American South, rice and tobacco were shipped abroad. For the western farmers, the Mississippi River served as the gateway to New Orleans and foreign trade.

As a result, trade and shipping were booming. In 1790, American ships had carried less than 50 percent of the commerce between the United States and Great Britain, its main customer. But by 1800, American ships carried almost all of it, 95 percent. In 1790, 246 American ships had arrived in British ports, carrying 45,000 tons of merchandise. Ten years later, 550 American ships arrived there, with 124,000 tons. It was no wonder, therefore, that freedom of the seas was a major political issue between the United States and foreign countries.

In those days before the income tax was even thought of, the United States government raised most of the money it needed from customs duties. This tax on imports brought in $4.4 million during 1791, when it provided virtually all the federal income. That year, the government spent $3.1 million, as follows: $633,000 for the army, $1.2 million to pay off debts, and $1.3 million for salaries, fighting Indians, pensions, and foreign affairs. Today, with the annual budget of the United States running into hundreds of billions of dollars, such small sums would operate the government only for a minute or two.

Now that the debt of the United States has reached trillions of dollars, it may be surprising to look at the balance sheet of the nation during its formative years. All the figures below are in millions of dollars.

YEAR	REVENUE	EXPENDITURE	SURPLUS	DEFICIT
1791	$4.4	$3.1	$1.3	
1792	3.7	6.2		$2.5
1793	4.6	3.8	.8	
1794	5.4	6.2		.8
1795	6.1	7.3		1.2
1796	8.4	5.8	2.6	

President Washington himself, delivering his annual address to Congress at the end of 1795, gave a rosy picture of the state of the nation:

> I trust I do not deceive myself when I indulge the persuasion that I have never met you at any period when more than at the present the situation of our public affairs has afforded just cause for mutual congratulation . . . [I invite] you to join with me in profound gratitude to the Author of all Good for the numerous and extraordinary blessings we enjoy.

Then Washington proceeded to list those blessings. First of all, he said, General Wayne's victory over the Indians at the Battle of Fallen Timbers promised peace in the Northwest between settlers and the Indians. In the Mediterranean, negotiations were under way to neutralize the Barbary pirates who were molesting American ships. In Madrid, a treaty with Spain that would open up the port of New Orleans was near completion. And he cited his signing of the controversial Jay Treaty with Great Britain as further evidence of peaceful foreign relations.

Turning to domestic affairs, Washington contrasted tur-

Charles Balthazar Julien Ferret de Saint-Mémin was the last artist to draw George Washington from life. His crayon drawing was executed in November 1789, when Washington had come to Philadelphia to help organize the nation against possible hostilities with France. Original work lost. *Picture Collection of the New York Public Library.*

moil abroad with serenity at home. "While many of the nations of Europe, with their American dependencies, have
been involved in a contest unusually bloody, exhausting and
calamitous, in which the evils of foreign war have been ag-
gravated by domestic convulsion and insurrection," he said,
"our favored country, happy in striking contrast, has enjoyed
a general tranquillity."

But Washington was actually setting another pattern for
future presidents by this overly optimistic assessment of the
accomplishments of his administration. Among the serious
problems he glossed over were the rising tension between
the United States and France, along with increasing political
turmoil at home. As partisan feelings had become more violent, even Washington himself was no longer immune to
personal attacks—a fact referred to in an account of his address printed by a newspaper called *Porcupine's Gazette.*

First the writer, obviously a Washington supporter, commented that the president was "a timid speaker" proving
that "superior genius, wisdom and courage are ever accompanied with excessive modesty." But then the report continued:

> His situation was at this time almost entirely new. Never, till
> a few months preceding this session, had the tongue of the
> most factious slander dared to make a public attack on his
> character. This was the first time he had entered the walls of
> Congress without a full assurance of meeting a welcome from
> every heart.

Washington privately felt angry at the attacks upon him.
He wrote to Jefferson that he found it hard to believe that "I
should be accused of being the enemy of one nation, and
subject to the influence of another; and to prove it, that
every act of my administration would be tortured, and the

grossest misrepresentations of them be made (and giving one side only of a subject), and that too in such exaggerated and indecent terms as could scarcely be applied to a Nero, a notorious defaulter, or a common pickpocket."

But 1796 was an election year and, as all subsequent chief executives would discover, politics spares not even the most respected president at such a time. Moreover, a retiring president finds that his powers of persuasion diminish as his term draws to a close. Even George Washington had that experience when it came to replacing members of his cabinet.

The resignation of Edmund Randolph as secretary of state left Washington with a key vacancy. To his shock, he found that no one wanted the job. He offered it to William Paterson of New Jersey, who declined. Former Governor Thomas Johnson of Maryland also refused, as did Charles Cotesworth Pinckney of South Carolina. Then Washington turned to Patrick Henry of Virginia, who refused, too.

Washington sought help from Alexander Hamilton, asking him to find out whether Rufus King, a Federalist senator from New York, would accept. Hamilton wrote back that King declined, too, because of "the disgust which a virtuous and independent mind" felt at the prospect of becoming a target for "foul and venomous shafts of calumny."

Hamilton added: "I wish, sir, I could present to you any useful ideas as a substitute, but the embarrassment is extreme as to the Secretary of State. In fact, a first rate character is not attainable. A second rate must be taken with good dispositions and barely decent qualifications. I wish I could throw more light. 'Tis a sad omen for the government."

Finally, in desperation, Washington turned to Timothy Pickering of Massachusetts, the secretary of war, who had been acting as secretary of state, too—and Pickering accepted the more prestigious post. That left a vacancy in the War Department. To fill it, Washington selected a former aide, James McHenry of Maryland, an Irish-born physician who had served as his secretary for a time during the Revolutionary War. McHenry is remembered today not for anything he did as secretary of war, but because Fort McHenry in Baltimore harbor, named after him, was the scene of a rocket bombardment by the British during the War of 1812 that led Francis Scott Key to write "The Star-Spangled Banner."

Observing Washington's difficulties with cabinet appointments, Vice President Adams commented, "The offices are once more filled, but how differently than when Jefferson, Hamilton, Jay, etc., were here!"

Washington also had a problem finding a new leader for the Supreme Court because John Jay, the chief justice, upon his return from his treaty-making mission to London, learned that he had been elected governor of New York. Accordingly, he resigned his judicial post. On July 1, 1795, Washington appointed John Rutledge of South Carolina to take Jay's place. Rutledge took the oath of office in August and presided at the court sessions—but only until the Senate reconvened in December.

Then, he, too, became a victim of the extreme political passions that the Jay Treaty had aroused. Even though he was a strong Federalist and a supporter of Washington, Rutledge, like many southerners, opposed the Jay Treaty. According to one writer, Rutledge, somewhat demented by the recent death of his wife, "ranted and raved on the streets of Charleston in denunciation of the treaty." When the Senate met to consider his confirmation as chief justice, it voted fourteen to ten against him. It was the first time the Senate refused to confirm a presidential appointment to the Supreme Court—a rare occurrence that has been repeated in our own time in the administrations of Presidents Lyndon B. Johnson, Richard M. Nixon, and Ronald Reagan.

But President Washington had even more trouble. In January of 1796, he appointed William Cushing of Massachusetts, then an associate justice, to be chief justice. Although Cushing was confirmed by the Senate without any problem, he declined to serve, saying he preferred to remain an associate justice. Then Washington turned to Senator Oliver Ellsworth of Massachusetts, who was quickly confirmed as chief justice, taking office on March 4, 1796.

A few days later, Washington appeared to be cheerful again. Vice President Adams, writing to his wife, told her that Washington had drawn him aside at a dinner party and talked politics to him, a most unusual occurrence. "He gave me intimations that his reign would be very short," Adams wrote. "He repeated it three times at least, that this and that was of no consequence to him personally, as he had but a very little while to stay in his present situation."

In June, Washington went to Mount Vernon, but he returned to Philadelphia in August. He was ready then to publish a farewell address to the American people, prepared with the help of Alexander Hamilton. In those days before television and radio, the only means of communication between the president and the people was the press. So Washington asked David C. Claypoole, publisher of *Claypoole's American Daily Advertiser*, to call upon him, and Claypoole later reported what happened.

Seated in his drawing room, Washington told Claypoole that he contemplated retiring from public life and had several "thoughts and reflections" for the American people— and that he had selected the *Advertiser* to print his statement. Of course, the prospect of publishing an exclusive report of the president's words was most pleasing to Claypoole. They agreed that the president's message would be printed on Monday, September 17.

"After the proof sheet had been carefully compared with the copy and corrected by myself," Claypoole wrote, "I carried two different revises to be examined by the President, who made but few alterations from the original, except in punctuation, in which he was very minute . . . I waited on the President with the original, and in presenting it to him, expressed my regret at parting with it, and how much I would be gratified at being permitted to retain it, upon which in the most obliging manner, he handed it back to me, saying that if I wished for it, I might keep it."*

Almost two-thirds of the farewell address was devoted to domestic affairs, but it is remembered today mainly because of the first president's advice on foreign affairs. He warned the American people against any sectional policy based on geographical distinctions, and, as he had repeatedly done in the past, warned against excessive party spirit, which he thought tended to divide Americans and possibly make them tools of European powers. Then Washington came to the heart of his message:

Europe has a set of primary interests which to us have none or a very remote relation. Hence she must be engaged in frequent controversies, the causes of which are essentially foreign to our concerns . . . Our detached and distant situation invites and enables us to pursue a different course . . . It is our true policy to steer clear of permanent alliances with any portion of the foreign world . . . taking care always to keep ourselves by suitable establishments on a respectable

*The original copy of Washington's farewell address now belongs to the New York Public Library.

defensive posture, we may safely trust to temporary alliances for extraordinary emergencies.

During the final months of the Washington administration, the nation's attention focused on the impending presidential election: Who would succeed Washington? Would it be John Adams, the Federalist candidate, or Thomas Jefferson, the Democratic-Republican candidate? In contrast to the long and highly publicized elections of today, the candidates then did not campaign at all. They did not make speeches, appear in public, issue platforms, accept financial contributions, or do anything to forward their own cause. Nor did Washington himself take any position for or against either candidate.

The results of the election showed a nation almost equally split between Federalists and Democratic-Republicans. Adams received seventy-one electoral votes to Jefferson's sixty-eight, so Adams became the nation's second president, with Jefferson the vice president. While Washington may have been "the indispensable man" at the time of the establishment of the new government, eight years later the nation was strong enough so that other men could carry on.

When Adams took the oath of office on March 4, 1797, many members of the audience felt their eyes wet with tears as they watched the heroic Washington formally depart from public life. Washington himself sat on one side of the dais, dressed in an old-fashioned black coat, without showing any emotion. But as Adams looked around, he thought he saw an expression on Washington's face that he later described in a letter to his wife:

> He seemed to me to enjoy a triumph over me. Methought I heard him say, 'Ay, I am fairly out and you fairly in! See which one will be happiest!'

Following a dinner in his honor, Washington left Philadelphia for Mount Vernon. But the peaceful retirement on his farm that he had so long looked forward to unfortunately proved of short duration. Less than three years later, he came in from a ride around his property complaining of a sore throat. After a brief illness, Washington died at Mount Vernon on December 14, 1799, at the age of sixty-seven.

In his own era, Washington had not been universally admired. Despite the high regard most Americans felt for him, when he retired the *Philadelphia Aurora*, for instance, wrote: "This day ought to be a jubilee in the United States . . . for the man who is the source of all misfortune of our country, is this day reduced to a level with his fellow citizens." But the verdict of history is quite the opposite.

Now nobody denies that George Washington was truly the indispensable man during the formative years of the United States. According to the noted historian Samuel Eliot Morison, "His unique place in history rests not only on his superb leadership in war, and on his wise administration of the federal government, but even more on his integrity, good judgment, and magnanimity."

For Washington left behind a government that had been firmly established. During its first eight years, the "frail fabric" of the Constitution, as Hamilton had called it, had withstood every test. Washington—along with Madison, Hamilton, Jefferson, and many other lesser-known figures— had breathed life into the words of the Constitution, creating a new kind of government that has not only survived but thrived remarkably.

Two hundred years later, the federal government brought into existence by Washington and his colleagues faces awesome problems that the Founding Fathers could scarcely have imagined. The example they set shows how individuals of integrity and good will can achieve great aims—and so their accomplishments continue to inspire the forces of democracy everywhere.

A CHRONOLOGY

Following is a chronology of important events in the first years of the United States government:

1789

FEBRUARY 4—Electors meet in state capitals and vote for George Washington as president, John Adams as vice president.

MARCH 4—Only thirteen members of the House of Representatives and eight senators appear on the date set for Congress to meet, so both chambers adjourn to await a quorum.

APRIL 1—First quorum in House of Representatives. Frederick Augustus Muhlenberg elected Speaker of the House.

6—First quorum in Senate. John Langdon elected president pro tem. Electoral votes counted in joint session of House and Senate.

7—Senate appoints a committee headed by Oliver Ellsworth to write its rules of procedure, and also appoints him chairman of committee to write a bill for the judiciary.

8—James Madison introduces a bill in the House to levy a duty on goods and merchandise imported into the United States.

9—John Adams notified of his election as vice president.

14—George Washington notified of his election as president.

16—Washington leaves Mount Vernon to take up his duties as president.

21—John Adams is introduced to the Senate and takes his seat as the presiding officer.

23—Washington arrives in New York City.

30—Washington is inaugurated as president and John Adams as vice president.

MAY 1—Washington holds his first reception for federal and state officials.

6—Washington makes his first public appearance as president at graduation exercises of Columbia College.

7—Washington attends the first inaugural ball, held in the Assembly Room on Lower Broadway.

14—Congress decides to call Washington "the President of the United States," as provided for in the Constitution, adding no other title.

25—The Senate considers its first message from the president, on negotiations by the governor of the Western Territories with Indians.

27—Martha Washington arrives in New York City.

JUNE 1—President Washington signs the first law passed by Congress, prescribing oaths to be taken by officers of the federal government. Congress concludes first United States treaty with an Indian tribe.

5—Martha Washington makes her first public appearance, attending a theater with her husband.

8—James Madison proposes a bill of rights in the House.

12—The Senate agrees with the House on bill to levy duties on imports.

15—Washington submits his first appointment to the

Senate for confirmation, that of William Short to
be chargé d'affaires in Paris.

20—Washington undergoes surgery to drain an abscess on his leg.

JULY 4—Washington signs first tariff bill, placing a duty on
imports.

27—Washington signs bill creating Department of
Foreign Affairs, whose name is soon changed to
Department of State.

AUGUST 3—Washington submits names of 102 nominees for
various federal jobs, such as customs collectors.

4—Senate rejects Washington's nomination of Benjamin Fishbourne to be federal officer of the port
of Savannah.

7—Washington signs act establishing Department of
War.

22—Washington appears in Senate chambers to ask its
advice and consent on a treaty with Indians.

SEPTEMBER 2—Washington signs bill establishing Department of
the Treasury.

11—Alexander Hamilton, the first secretary of the
treasury, takes office.

12—Henry Knox takes office as the first secretary of
war.

22—Washington signs bill creating Post Office Department, under the secretary of the treasury.

24—Washington signs judiciary bill, creating a Supreme Court, district courts, and circuit courts,
as well as establishing the office of Attorney General, and he appoints John Jay the first chief justice.

25—Both houses of Congress pass the Bill of Rights.

26—Washington appoints Thomas Jefferson the first
secretary of state, and he appoints Edmund Randolph the first attorney general. Samuel Osgood
takes the oath of office as the first postmaster
general.

29—Washington signs the first appropriation bill passed by Congress, providing $629,000 for salaries, War Department bills, and veterans' pensions. First session of first Congress adjourns.

OCTOBER 3—Washington issues first proclamation for a day of Thanksgiving, to be held on Thursday, November 26.

15—Washington departs on a month's tour of New England.

NOVEMBER 20—New Jersey becomes first state to ratify the Bill of Rights.

21—North Carolina ratifies the Constitution, becoming the nation's twelfth state.

26—Nation celebrates first Thanksgiving Day.

DECEMBER 19—Maryland ratifies the Bill of Rights.

22—North Carolina ratifies the Bill of Rights.

1790

JANUARY 1—Martha Washington holds her first New Year's Day reception.

7—Second session of first Congress opens.

8—Washington delivers first State of the Union address to Congress.

14—Hamilton delivers his "Report on the Public Credit" to Congress.

19—South Carolina ratifies Bill of Rights.

25—New Hampshire ratifies Bill of Rights.

28—House of Representatives begins debate on Hamilton's "Report on Public Credit." Delaware ratifies Bill of Rights.

FEBRUARY 1—First session of Supreme Court held but lacks a quorum.

2—First official session of Supreme Court held.

22—Washington holds his first birthday reception as president. Congress passes law calling for the nation's first census.

23—President and Mrs. Washington move to a new home in New York, from No. 1 Cherry Street to Macomb Mansion on Broadway.

27—New York ratifies Bill of Rights.

MARCH 10—Pennsylvania ratifies Bill of Rights.

22—Jefferson takes oath of office as first secretary of state.

APRIL 10—Nation's first patent law passed.

MAY 29—Rhode Island ratifies the Constitution, the last of the original thirteen states to do so.

31—Washington signs nation's first copyright bill.

JUNE 7—Rhode Island ratifies the Bill of Rights.

JULY 16—Congress passes law locating seat of government on the Potomac River, as a result of political deal between Hamilton and Jefferson.

AUGUST 1—Nation's first census begins.

4—Congress passes Hamilton's proposed funding act.

5—Board of Assumption of Debts created, with federal government taking over $21.5 million of state debts.

12—Second session of first Congress adjourns.

13—Washington signs Treaty of New York with the Creek Indians.

30—Washington leaves New York as government starts move to Philadelphia.

NOVEMBER 22—Washington leaves Mount Vernon for Philadelphia.

27—Washington arrives in Philadelphia.

DECEMBER 6—Third session of first Congress meets in Philadelphia.

8—Washington delivers his second State of the Union message.

13—Hamilton recommends establishing a national bank.

1791

JANUARY 10—Vermont ratifies the Constitution.

FEBRUARY 25—Washington signs bill granting a charter to the Bank of the United States.

MARCH 4—Arthur St. Clair named as commanding general of forces against the Indians of the Northwest Territory. Vermont admitted as the fourteenth state.

APRIL 7—Washington leaves on a tour of the southern states.

OCTOBER 24—First session of second Congress opens.

NOVEMBER 4—St. Clair defeated by Indians on the Wabash.

DECEMBER 15—The Bill of Rights declared ratified.

1792

APRIL 2—Washington signs bill creating a mint to coin money.

5—Washington vetoes his first bill, one to reapportion seats in the House of Representatives.

JUNE 1—Kentucky ratifies Constitution and is admitted as the fifteenth state.

SEPTEMBER 15—Washington issues a proclamation warning citizens not to resist paying excise tax on whiskey.

DECEMBER 5—Electors in various states cast their ballots for president.

1793

FEBRUARY 13—Congress tabulates electoral votes and declares Washington reelected as president and Adams as vice president.

MARCH 3—Results of first census set the population of the United States at 3,929,204.

4—Washington inaugurated for second term, in Philadelphia.

APRIL 22—Washington issues proclamation of neutrality in the war between France and England.

MAY 18—Washington receives Citizen Genêt as the new French minister.

AUGUST 1—Washington asks French government to recall Genêt.

SEPTEMBER 10—Washington leaves for Mount Vernon after yellow fever epidemic breaks out in Philadelphia.

18—Washington participates in laying cornerstone for Capitol Building in new federal city on the Potomac.

DECEMBER 31—Resignation of Thomas Jefferson as secretary of state becomes effective.

1794

JANUARY 2—Edmund Randolph takes office as secretary of state.

MARCH 5—Eleventh Amendment to Constitution submitted to the states for ratification.

APRIL 16—Washington nominates John Jay, the chief justice, to be special envoy to England to negotiate a treaty.

JUNE 5—Washington signs a bill proclaiming neutrality in the European war.

JULY 16—Whiskey Rebellion breaks out in western Pennsylvania.

AUGUST 7—Washington issues a proclamation ordering Whiskey Rebellion protesters to disperse and calls out militia.

20—General Anthony Wayne defeats Indians at the Battle of Fallen Timbers.

SEPTEMBER 30—Washington leaves for Carlisle, Pennsylvania, to inspect troops called to suppress Whiskey Rebellion.

NOVEMBER 19—In London, John Jay signs a treaty with England, by which England agrees to yield its forts in the Northwest Territory.

DECEMBER 1—Hamilton resigns as secretary of the treasury.
31—Knox resigns as secretary of war.

1795

JANUARY 2—Timothy Pickering becomes secretary of war.

FEBRUARY 3—Oliver Wolcott becomes secretary of the treasury.
7—Eleventh Amendment to the Constitution ratified.

MARCH 8—Washington submits the Jay Treaty to Senate for ratification.

JUNE 24—Jay Treaty ratified.
29—Jay resigns as chief justice.

JULY 10—Washington issues proclamation pardoning those who participated in the Whiskey Rebellion.

AUGUST 3—Treaty of Greenville signed, under which Indians yield two-thirds of Ohio to white settlement.
19—Washington summons Randolph to explain letter sent by the French minister.
20—Randolph resigns as secretary of state.

SEPTEMBER 5—Treaty of peace signed with Algiers, leading to the release of some prisoners captured by the Barbary pirates.

OCTOBER 27—Thomas Pinckney negotiates a treaty with Spain, opening the port of New Orleans to American trade.

DECEMBER 10—Timothy Pickering takes oath of office as third secretary of state, and Charles Lee as the third attorney general.

1796

JANUARY 27—James McHenry takes office as the third secretary of war.

MARCH 3—Washington appoints Oliver Ellsworth chief justice.

30—Washington refuses to release papers about the Jay Treaty to the House of Representatives.

JUNE 1—Tennessee admitted as the sixteenth state.

SEPTEMBER 17—Washington issues his Farewell Address.

NOVEMBER 4—Treaty of peace signed with Tripoli.

DECEMBER 7—Presidential electors cast their ballots, electing John Adams the second president and Thomas Jefferson the vice president.

1797

MARCH 4—Adams inaugurated as president.

A NOTE ON SOURCES
AND BIBLIOGRAPHY

When we finished our book on the Constitution, *We the People, the Story of the United States Constitution Since* 1789, we began to wonder how the Founding Fathers created a government from that document. What did they do, and how did they do it?

We began our research at the National Archives and the Library of Congress in Washington, D.C., where many of the original papers of the early government are available to scholars. Then we read scores of books by historians and political scientists about the first days of the United States. For their help in obtaining some of those books, we would like to thank the librarians at the Pine Plains Free Library, Pine Plains, New York; the Vassar College Library, Poughkeepsie, New York; the Columbia-Greene Community College Library, Hudson, New York; and the New York State Library, Albany, New York.

Most of the scholarly books about that early period are far too detailed for the general reader. So we have selected a few that are both readable and reliable, for those who want to dig a little deeper into the birth of the United States.

Boller, Paul F., Jr. *Presidential Campaigns*. New York: Oxford, 1984.

Bower, Catherine Drinker. *Miracle at Philadelphia*. Boston: Little, Brown, 1966.

Bowers, Claude G. *Jefferson and Hamilton*. Boston: Houghton Mifflin, 1925.

Caughey, John Walton. *McGillivray of the Creeks*. Norman: University of Oklahoma, 1938.

Faber, Doris. *John Jay*. New York: G. P. Putnam's Sons, 1966.

Faber, Doris, and Harold Faber. *We the People, the Story of the United States Constitution Since 1789*. New York: Charles Scribner's Sons, 1987.

Faber, Harold. *From Sea to Sea: The Growth of the United States*. New York: Farrar, Strauss & Geroux, 1967.

Flexner, James Thomas. *George Washington and the New Nation* (1783–1793). Boston: Little, Brown, 1970.

Freeman, Douglas Southall. *George Washington, Patriot and President*, 1784–1793. Vol. 6. New York: Charles Scribner's Sons, 1954.

Hart, James. *The American Presidency in Action*, 1789. New York: Macmillan, 1948.

McDonald, Forrest. *The Presidency of George Washington*. Lawrence: University of Kansas, 1974.

Maclay, Edgar S., ed. *Journal of William Maclay*. New York: D. Appleton and Co., 1890.

Miller, John C. *The Federalist Era*, 1789–1801. New York: Harper & Row, 1960.

Morris, Richard B. *Seven Who Shaped Our Destiny*. New York: Harper & Row, 1973.

National Archives and Record Service. *The Story of the Bill of Rights*. Washington, D.C.: The National Archives and Record Service, 1980.

Smith, Thomas E. V. *The City of New York in the Year of Washington's Inauguration*. Riverside, Calif.: Chatham Press, 1972.

Tebbel, John. *George Washington's America*. New York: E. P. Dutton, 1954.

INDEX

Adams, Abigail, 34, 56, 114
Adams, John, 172, 173, 175
  background of, 34–35
  in presidential title debate,
    34–36, 38–40
  reelection of, 108
  in 1796 elections, 175
  as vice president, 18–19, 30, 45
agrarian interests, 100–101
agricultural production, 167
Algiers, 149, 150–153, 154
Alliance Treaty (1778), 137
American Revolution, *see*
  Revolutionary War
Ames, Fisher, 17, 20, 30, 86
Anti-Federalists, 14, 16, 89–91,
  99–100
  Madison's leadership of, 101
appointments, presidential, 44–45,
  48–49
army, U.S., 42, 43

Indians and, 131–134
  in Whiskey Rebellion, 160–163
Arnold, Benedict, 110
Attorney General, U.S., 43–44

Bainbridge, William, 154
Bank of the United States, 100–104
Bard, Samuel, 59
Barlow, Joel, 152–153
Barnum, P. T., 114
Betsy, capture of, 150
Bill of Rights, 63–66, 99–100
Bingham, Anne Willing, 114–115
Bingham, William, 114
Black Wolf, Chief, 134
Blair, John, 76
Blue Jacket, Chief, 134
Board of Treasury, 43, 48
Brackenridge, Hugh Henry,
  157–158, 161
Bradford, David, 158, 162